Carnivore Cuisine

A Guide to Delicious Meat-Based Recipes

Meal Plan Included for a Balanced Carnivorous Diet

Paul Warren

Copyright © 2023 - All rights reserved.

The content contained within this book may not be reproduced, duplicated, or transmitted without direct written permission from the author or the publisher.

Under no circumstances will any blame or legal responsibility be held against the publisher, or author, for any damages, reparation, or monetary loss due to the information contained within this book. Either directly or indirectly.

Legal Notice: This book is copyright protected. This book is only for personal use. You cannot amend, distribute, sell, use, quote, or paraphrase any part, or the content within this book, without the consent of the author or publisher.

Disclaimer Notice: Please note the information contained within this document is for educational and entertainment purposes only. All effort has been executed to present accurate, up-to-date, and reliable, complete information. No warranties of any kind are declared or implied. Readers acknowledge that the author is not engaging in the rendering of legal, financial, medical, or professional advice. The content within this book has been derived from various sources. Please consult a licensed professional before attempting any techniques outlined in this book.

By reading this document, the reader agrees that under no circumstances is the author responsible for any losses, direct or indirect, which are incurred as a result of the use of the information contained within this document, including, but not limited to, — errors, omissions, or inaccuracies.

Table of Contents

Classic Carnivore Breakfasts

Bacon and Eggs

A popular and well-liked continental breakfast that is incredibly satisfying and tasty is bacon and eggs. It is one of the finest Keto breakfasts.

Serving Size: 4

Ingredients:

- 8 egg
- Salt as needed
- 1/2 c. cherry tomatoes
- 1/4 c. parsley
- 150 g. bacon
- Black pepper, as required

Instructions:

1. Cook the bacon in a skillet. Cook until crispy in a skillet over medium-low heat.
2. Cook the eggs and cherry tomatoes in a skillet. Eggs can be cooked in the same pan as the potatoes. Cover the pan to ensure thorough egg cooking. Cherry tomatoes are cut into slices and cooked in the pan simultaneously.
3. Arrange seasoned eggs and bacon on the plate.
4. Season with salt and pepper, and garnish with fresh parsley. Serve with piping-hot eggs and bacon.

Steak and Eggs

Keep things simple with steak and eggs! Combine your favorite steak with eggs cooked to perfection.

Serving Size: 2 | Duration: 25 minutes

Ingredients:

For the Eggs and steak:

- 6 oz. bone-in rib-eye/sirloin steak
- Salt and freshly ground black pepper
- 2 tbsp. unsalted butter
- 2 big free-range eggs

For the optional Chimichurri Steak Garnish:

- 1/4 c. chopped flat-leaf parsley
- A few red pepper flakes
- 1/4 c. virgin olive oil
- 1/4 c. chopped oregano
- 4 sprigs of fresh mint
- Juice of 1/2 lime
- 2 garlic cloves minced
- Salt and freshly ground black pepper

Instruction:

For the Chimichurri:

1. In a medium mixing bowl, combine all of the ingredients. Set aside the proteins after they have finished cooking.

For the Steak and Eggs:

1. In a large cast-iron skillet over medium-high heat, melt the butter. Arrange the steak on one side of the grill, leaving room for the eggs.
2. Cook for 3 to 4 minutes on each side for a medium-rare steak or until the meat has a dark brown sear.
3. If the pan begins to dry out, add another tablespoon of butter. After lowering the heat, add the eggs.
4. Season with salt and pepper to taste. Cover the skillet with a lid and cook the egg whites for another 2 to 3 minutes or until

they start to set.

5. Season the meat with salt and pepper before serving it with the eggs.

6. Serve with or without the chimichurri sauce.

Sausage and Eggs

What could be better for breakfast than hot, crispy sausages with scrambled eggs? Because it is high in nutrition, this is an excellent meal to prepare when running late for work.

Serving Size: 1

Ingredients:

- 2 tbsp. Butter
- 2 sausages
- A pinch of salt
- 2 eggs

Instructions:

1. Bring some water to a boil. Allow 8-10 minutes in boiling water after adding the eggs.
2. Grill or fry the sausages while the eggs are boiling. Remove the eggs from the water and peel them.
3. Scramble the eggs with a fork, then add the butter and salt.
4. Slice the sausages into small pieces. Dig into the mashed eggs with sausages!

Ham and Eggs

The American staple pairing of ham and cheese is popular. Sadly, ham and egg dishes don't have the same popularity but are fantastic. They are as delectable and versatile as ham and cheese.

You may prepare omelets, burritos, ham and egg breakfasts, and more!

Total Time: 20 minutes | Servings: 4

Ingredients:

- 8 eggs, beaten
- 1/4 tsp. seasoned salt
- 3 tbsp. milk
- 1 jalapeno pepper, seeded and minced
- Salt and ground black pepper
- 1/4 c. olive oil
- 1/2 c. chopped deli slices Applewood-smoked ham
- 1 c. finely shredded Cheddar cheese, divided

Instruction:

1. Mix the eggs, milk, seasoned salt, and black pepper in a bowl.
2. Heat the olive oil in a large nonstick skillet over medium-high heat for two to three minutes or until the jalapeno pepper softens. Cook for about a minute, or until the ham is cooked through, with the jalapeno.
3. Pour the egg mixture into the ham mixture. Cook for 3-5 minutes or until the eggs are set but not dry. Sprinkle half of the cheddar cheese over the eggs; cook and stir until the cheese is melted. Then, on a plate, top the eggs with the remaining cheese.

Breakfast Steak Burrito

This dish may be prepared in only 20 minutes without sacrificing any flavor. The meal is "customizable" and contains fresh, juicy steak in every bite!

Ingredients:

- 1/2 c. prepared salsa
- 1/2 c. water
- 1/4 c. instant brown rice
- 1 15-ounce can of black beans, low-sodium, rinsed
- 12 oz. steak, thinly sliced crosswise
- 1/4 tsp. newly ground pepper
- 2 tbsp. chopped fresh cilantro
- 1 tbsp. canola oil
- 1/2 c. shredded Cheddar cheese
- 4 8-inch tortillas, whole-wheat preferred
- 1/4 c. prepared guacamole

Instructions:

1. Bring salsa and water to a boil in a small saucepan.
2. Reduce to low heat, cover, and cook for 5 minutes.
3. Return to a simmer and cook for 5 minutes, uncovered, or until the rice is tender and most liquid has been absorbed.
4. Meanwhile, season the meat with pepper. Heat the oil in a large skillet over medium-high heat. Cook, occasionally tossing, for 3-5 minutes or until the steak is browned and cooked.
5. Divide the steak between the tortillas and top with an equal amount of cheese, guacamole, cilantro, and rice mixture. Each tortilla should be used to make a burrito.

Carnivore Omelet

In just 15 minutes, you can finish cooking a carnivorous omelet with various topping options. You name it—cheese, bacon, yogurt! So, don't restrict the enjoyment to only the morning; enjoy the high-protein breakfast anytime.

Ingredients:

- 4 large Eggs
- 50 g. Greek Yogurt
- 1 piece Bacon
- 50 g. 20% Beef Mince / Ground
- 20 g. Mozzarella Cheese
- 20 g. Salami
- 1/2 tsp. Himalayan Sea Salt

Instructions:

1. Brown the mince and bacon in a skillet heated to medium heat with some light oil.
2. Meanwhile, beat the eggs.
3. After the meat has finished cooking, remove them and add the eggs.
4. Tilt the pan occasionally to help the runny portions settle in the center. Once the egg has started to firm up, add the toppings.
5. Cook for a few minutes more, then remove, fold, and serve.

Bacon and Egg Breakfast Salad

Eggs are abundant in protein and strong in minerals, vitamins, and antioxidants. Hence, if consumed in moderation, bacon and eggs may be a healthy breakfast meal.

Ingredients:

- 1 tsp. garlic oil
- 4 eggs
- 1 head escarole/frisee/other bitter leaves of choice
- 7 oz. smoked lardoons or about 14 slices of smoked bacon (cut into chunks)
- A dash of Worcestershire sauce

- 1 tsp. Dijon mustard
- 4 tsp. cider vinegar
- Small bunch of flat-leaf parsley, chop leaves

Instructions:

1. Boil the eggs in a saucepan of water over medium heat. Bring to a boil, cook for one minute, then remove from heat and set aside for ten minutes.
2. Chill the eggs in a dish of ice water. Peel the eggs once they are cool to the touch.
3. Meanwhile, tear the salad leaves into bite-sized pieces and place them in a serving bowl.
4. Heat the oil in a small frying pan over medium heat. Fry the lardons or bacon for 5 minutes or until crisp. Transfer the lardons or bacon to a plate lined with paper towels to drain while you make the dressing.
5. After whisking together the Dijon mustard and bacon juices in the pan, add the vinegar and a dab of Worcestershire sauce. Re-whisk the dressing before pouring it over the salad greens and tossing to combine.
6. Combine the eggs with the chopped parsley, add the lardons, and mix again. When gently mixing the ingredients, do not break up the eggs.
7. Hard-boiled eggs can be made four days ahead of time. Cool, keep the shells on, and store them in an airtight container in the fridge. Remove the shells just before serving.

Chorizo and Egg Breakfast Bowl

Breakfast bowls are fantastic, but many dishes can leave you hungry and wanting more. The ultimate comfort food meal is these chorizo breakfast bowls. This breakfast bowl is loaded with protein-rich quinoa, savory chorizo, fluffy eggs, and any toppings you like.

Ingredients:

- 1 tbsp. olive oil
- 1 c. quinoa
- 4 large eggs, lightly beaten
- 4 oz. chorizo see notes
- 1/2 c. diced yellow onion
- 2 garlic cloves minced
- 1 c. diced Roma tomatoes or your favorite tomatoes

Instructions:

1. In a large saucepan, cook the quinoa according to the package directions.
2. Over medium heat, heat the olive oil. Add the scrambled eggs when the olive oil is hot and cook until done. After removing from the pan, place on a plate.
3. Raise the heat to medium-high and cook the onions and garlic for 1 to 2 minutes or until tender.
4. Cook for 5 to 7 minutes, stirring frequently, until the chorizo is thoroughly cooked. If necessary, drain any excess fat.
5. Assemble the breakfast bowls.
6. Place an equal amount of quinoa in each dish, followed by eggs and tomatoes.
7. If desired, top with additional toppings.

Carnivore Breakfast Pizza

Everyone enjoys pizza, right? It is incredibly simple to make, full of flavor and protein.

Ingredients:

- 1 Carnivore Flatbread baked in a 13×11-inch rectangle or oval
- A dash of salt
- 1/2 c. heavy cream

- 1 clove of garlic pressed or minced
- 1/2 c. shredded cheese mozzarella, cheddar, or gouda
- 1/2 c. sour cream
- 3 slices of bacon chopped and pan-fried

Instructions:

1. Bake the Carnivore Flatbread in a 13 x 11-inch rectangle or oval pan. After removing the baking sheet from the oven, leave it lined. Preheat the oven to 415°F.
2. Combine the heavy cream, garlic, and salt in a small bowl. Then stir in the cheese. Spread the ingredients on the pizza crust and add bacon on top.
3. Bake the pizza for 15 minutes or until the cheese is melted. Refrigerate any leftovers in an airtight container.

Notes:

- This crust is simple to make ahead of time. Make the pizza crust the night before and bake it for breakfast. Finally, all that remains to be done in the morning is to top it and bake it!
- Crispy bacon enhances the flavor of this morning's pizza, but other meats also work well.
- You may substitute cooked breakfast sausage, chopped deli ham, or a variety of meats.

Carnivore Breakfast Sandwich

A breakfast sandwich is a tried-and-true favorite. This breakfast sandwich is full of flavor, high in protein and fat, and will keep you satisfied for the rest of the day. Instead of a carb, two sausage patties are used as the structure to keep the egg and cheddar cheese inside. Don't be shy if you're looking for a quick Carnivorous breakfast idea!

Ingredients:

- 1 egg

- 2 Beef Sausage Patties
- 1 tsp. butter/bacon grease, if you have it
- 1 oz. cheddar cheese

Instructions:

1. In a large skillet over medium heat, melt the butter. Form the sausage into thin patties about half an inch thick and the size of your palm. Fry patties until golden on one side, then flip and cook for two to three minutes or until done.

2. If it doesn't bother you, fry 1 egg in the same pan as the rest of your ingredients. If not, assemble your carnivore breakfast sandwich in a separate pan with more butter. Keep the sauce and yolk runny. Place 1 sausage patty, a fried egg, a slice of cheese, and another sausage patty on a platter.

3. Enjoy! Sautéed spinach, tomato, or avocado slices could also be added.

Keto Carnivore Waffle

You crave variety occasionally when it comes to a strict, high-protein, low-carb diet like the ketogenic or carnivore diet. This carnivore diet adaptation of a classic breakfast recipe will quickly become a favorite.

Ingredients:

- 1 egg
- 1/3 c. mozzarella cheese
- 1/2 c. ground pork rinds
- 1 pinch of salt

Instructions:

1. Preheat the waffle maker to medium-high temperature. Combine the egg, cheese, ground pork rinds, and salt in a mixing bowl.

2. Adding ingredients to a carnivorous waffle

3. Spoon the pancake on top of the waffle. After 3-5 minutes of cooking in a closed waffle machine, the waffles should be golden brown and firm. Remove the pancake from the waffle maker and serve it to yourself.

Chicken

Grilled Chicken with Mango Salsa

Ingredients:

- 4 boneless, skinless chicken breasts
- 1 large ripe mango, peeled and diced
- 1/2 red onion, diced
- 1 red bell pepper, diced
- 1 jalapeño pepper, seeded and minced
- 1/4 cup chopped fresh cilantro
- 2 tbsp lime juice
- 1 tbsp honey
- 1 tbsp olive oil
- Salt and pepper

Instructions:

1. Preheat a grill to medium-high heat.
2. Brush the chicken breasts with olive oil and season with salt and pepper.
3. Grill the chicken for 5-6 minutes per side, or until it is cooked through.
4. While the chicken is grilling, prepare the mango salsa by mixing together the diced mango, red onion, red bell pepper, jalapeño pepper, cilantro, lime juice, honey, and a pinch of salt in a bowl.
5. Serve the grilled chicken with the mango salsa spooned over the top.

Chicken and Vegetable Stir-Fry

Ingredients:

- 1 lb boneless, skinless chicken breasts, cut into strips
- 1 red bell pepper, sliced

- 1 yellow onion, sliced
- 2 cups broccoli florets
- 3 cloves garlic, minced
- 2 tbsp soy sauce
- 1 tbsp cornstarch
- 1 tbsp vegetable oil

Instructions:

1. In a small bowl, mix together the soy sauce and cornstarch to make a sauce.
2. Heat the oil in a large skillet over medium-high heat. Add the chicken and cook until browned on all sides.
3. Add the garlic, red bell pepper, onion, and broccoli to the skillet and cook for a few minutes until the vegetables are tender-crisp.
4. Pour the sauce over the chicken and vegetables and stir to combine.
5. Cook for another minute or until the sauce thickens.
6. Serve the stir-fry over rice or noodles.

Lemon and Herb Grilled Chicken

Ingredients:

- 4 boneless, skinless chicken breasts
- 2 cloves garlic, minced
- 1/4 cup chopped fresh parsley
- 1/4 cup chopped fresh basil
- 2 tbsp olive oil
- 2 tbsp lemon juice
- 1 tsp lemon zest
- Salt and pepper

Instructions:

1. Preheat a grill to medium-high heat.
2. In a small bowl, mix together the garlic, parsley, basil, olive oil, lemon juice, lemon zest, salt, and pepper.
3. Brush the chicken breasts with the herb mixture and let them marinate for at least 30 minutes.
4. Grill the chicken for 5-6 minutes per side, or until it is cooked through.
5. Let the chicken rest for a few minutes before slicing it thinly against the grain.
6. Serve the grilled chicken with a side salad or grilled vegetables.

Chicken and Mushroom Risotto

Ingredients:

- 4 boneless, skinless chicken thighs, cut into cubes
- 8 oz mushrooms, sliced
- 1/2 cup chopped onion
- 1 1/2 cups Arborio rice
- 4 cups chicken broth
- 1/2 cup grated Parmesan cheese
- 2 tbsp butter
- 2 tbsp olive oil
- Salt and pepper

Instructions:

1. Heat the olive oil in a large skillet over medium-high heat. Add the chicken and cook until browned on all sides. Remove the chicken from the skillet and set aside.
2. Add the mushrooms and onion to the skillet and cook for a few minutes until the vegetables are tender.

3. Add the Arborio rice to the skillet and stir to coat it with the oil and vegetables.
4. Slowly pour the chicken broth into the skillet, stirring constantly to prevent lumps from forming.
5. Bring the mixture to a simmer and cook for 20-25 minutes, stirring occasionally, or until the rice is tender and the liquid has been absorbed.
6. Stir in the Parmesan cheese and butter until melted and well combined.
7. Return the chicken to the skillet and stir to combine.
8. Season with salt and pepper to taste.
9. Serve the risotto hot.

Grilled Chicken and Vegetable Kabobs

Ingredients:

- 4 boneless, skinless chicken breasts, cut into chunks
- 1 red bell pepper, cut into chunks
- 1 yellow onion, cut into chunks
- 2 zucchinis, sliced into rounds
- 2 tbsp olive oil
- 2 tbsp balsamic vinegar
- 2 cloves garlic, minced
- Salt and pepper

Instructions:

1. Soak wooden skewers in water for 30 minutes to prevent them from burning on the grill.
2. Thread the chicken and vegetables onto the skewers in any order you like.
3. In a small bowl, whisk together the olive oil, balsamic vinegar, garlic, salt, and pepper.

4. Brush the skewers with the oil mixture, making sure to coat all sides.
5. Preheat a grill to medium-high heat.
6. Grill the skewers for 8-10 minutes, turning occasionally, or until the chicken is cooked through.
7. Serve the skewers with a side salad or grilled vegetables.

Chicken Caesar Salad

Ingredients:

- 4 boneless, skinless chicken breasts
- 1 head of romaine lettuce, chopped
- 1/2 cup grated Parmesan cheese
- 1/2 cup croutons
- 1/4 cup Caesar salad dressing
- Salt and pepper

Instructions:

1. Preheat a grill to medium-high heat.
2. Brush the chicken breasts with olive oil and season with salt and pepper.
3. Grill the chicken for 5-6 minutes per side, or until it is cooked through.
4. Let the chicken rest for a few minutes before slicing it thinly against the grain.
5. In a large bowl, toss together the chopped romaine lettuce, Parmesan cheese, and croutons.
6. Drizzle the Caesar salad dressing over the salad and toss to coat.
7. Serve the salad topped with the sliced grilled chicken.

Fried Chicken

Chicken pieces are breaded and fried in hot oil until golden brown.

Total Time: 50 min | Yield: 16 pieces

Ingredients:

- 6 c. all-purpose flour
- Vegetable oil for frying
- 2 whole free-range, organic chickens
- 2 tsp. cayenne pepper
- 4 tbsp. ground black pepper
- 2 tbsp. garlic powder
- 5 tbsp. salt
- 1 tbsp. onion powder
- 2 c. buttermilk

Instructions:

1. Separate two whole chickens into four breasts, thighs, legs, and wings.
2. Preheat your oil to 325 degrees F in a deep fryer or a big stovetop pan.
3. Add the flour, salt, black pepper, garlic powder, onion powder, and cayenne pepper in a large mixing bowl. Place aside.
4. Place the buttermilk in a separate basin large enough to accommodate the chicken.
5. Prepare your dredging station. Place your chicken in a bowl. The buttermilk basin should be next to the dry mixture.
6. Lightly dust the chicken breasts with the flour mixture before dipping them in the buttermilk and covering them well.
7. Firmly press the flour mixture into the wet chicken breasts while holding the breasts in the flour mixture. The appropriate crust and crunch will not be obtained if the coating is not thoroughly applied. Carefully place the breasts in the hot oil.

8. Repeat the dredging procedures with the remaining chicken, starting with the thigh, then the leg, and finally, the wing.

9. When you add the last wing to the fryer, there should be 16 pieces of chicken in the oil. Set a timer for 15 minutes.

10. After 15 minutes, use a probe thermometer to check the temperature of a breast. If the thermometer reads 180 degrees F, your chicken is done. Remember that it will continue to cook after you remove it from the fryer. Set your chicken aside and let it drain for five minutes. Let cool before serving.

Chicken Alfredo

Pasta is tossed with a sauce made of cream, Parmesan cheese, and garlic and then topped with grilled chicken.

Ingredients:

- 1 1/2 c. whole milk
- 2 tbsp. extra-virgin olive oil
- Kosher salt
- Twp cloves garlic, minced
- Freshly ground black pepper
- 1 1/2 c. low-sodium chicken broth
- 1 c. freshly grated Parmesan
- Two boneless chicken breasts
- 8 oz. fettuccine
- 1/2 c. heavy cream
- Freshly chopped parsley

Instructions:

1. In a large skillet, heat the oil over medium-high heat. Season with salt and pepper to taste. Fry for 8 minutes per side or until golden and cooked through. Slice after 10 minutes of rest.

2. Combine the milk, broth, and garlic in a skillet. Cook the food after adding salt and pepper. Cook for 3 minutes, stirring regularly, after adding the fettuccine. Allow for another 8 minutes of simmering.

3. Stir in the heavy cream and Parmesan cheese. Simmer until the sauce thickens.

4. Remove from the heat and stir in the chicken slices. Garnish with parsley.

BBQ Chicken

Set your chicken aside and let it drain for five minutes. Let cool before serving.

Marinated chicken is grilled or baked with BBQ sauce. If done correctly, it will take at least an hour, if not two hours. Remember that, unlike grilling, which is hot and fast, BBQ is slow and low. Grilling a chicken breast is OK, but grilling chicken thighs, legs, or wings is preferable.

As a result, managing body heat in whatever way you can is critical. Place the chicken on the top rack of the grill, away from the heat, or if using a gas grill, just reduce the heat to low. You'll have a cool place either way. The greatest BBQ chicken is made slowly.

Total Time: 110 minutes | Servings: 4 to 6 servings

Ingredients:

- Kosher salt
- 4 lb. bone-in, skin-on chicken legs, wings, thighs, breasts
- 1 c. barbecue sauce, homemade or store-bought
- Vegetable oil or Extra virgin olive oil

Instructions:

1. Set your chicken aside and let it drain for five minutes. Let

cool before serving.

2. Season and oil the chicken pieces. The chicken pieces should be coated in olive oil and seasoned on all sides.

3. Preheat the grill. Set your grill to high; direct heat on one side. If you're using charcoal or wood, ensure the grill has a cold side with few to no embers.

4. Move the seared chicken to the cool side of the grill. Place the chicken pieces, skin side down, on the hotter side of the grill to sear the skin. Cook for 5 to 10 minutes without a cover to avoid scorching, depending on the grill's hotness.

5. Turn the chicken pieces over and place them on the cooler side of the grill once they have a decent sear on one side. Set your chicken aside and let it drain for five minutes. Let cool before serving.

6. If using a gas grill, move the chicken pieces to the colder side, away from the flame, and keep the flame only on one side of the grill. Reduce the temperature to low or mediumlow (250°F to 275°F).

7. Cook the grill, covered and without stirring, for 20 to 30 minutes. Cook, turn, and baste until done. Turn the chicken pieces over and baste with your favorite barbecue sauce. Cover the grill and cook for another 15 to 20 minutes.

8. Continue to flip the chicken pieces over, baste with sauce, cover the pan, and simmer for 10 to 30 minutes more. Set your chicken aside and let it drain for five minutes. Let cool before serving.

9. The timing will vary based on how your grill is set up, the size of your chicken pieces, and how chilly they start. Smaller pieces of chicken may finish cooking faster on a charcoal grill. The goal is to maintain the grill temperature low enough for the chicken to cook.

10. The internal temperature of the chicken pieces should be 160°F for the breasts and 170°F for the thighs when measured using a meat thermometer. The chicken is also done if the

fluids flow clear when a knife is placed into the thickest chunk.

11. Set your chicken aside and let it drain for five minutes. Let cool before serving. If the chicken hasn't finished cooking, turn it over and maintain the heat low.

12. Finish with a last sear on the hot side of the grill before removing it from the heat, if desired. Place the meat on the hot side of the grill, skin side down, to achieve this. Allow them to sear and blacken for a minute or two. Brush on more barbecue sauce to the grilled chicken before serving.

Chicken Parmesan

Breaded chicken cutlets are fried and baked with tomato sauce and mozzarella cheese.

Ingredients:

- 4 boneless, skinless chicken breast halves
- 2 large eggs
- Freshly ground black pepper and salt to taste
- 3/4 c. grated Parmesan cheese, divided
- 1 c. or as required of panko bread crumbs,
- 2 tbsp. or as required for all-purpose flour
- 1/2 c. of prepared tomato sauce
- 1/2 c. or required of olive oil
- 1/4 c. of chopped fresh basil
- 2 tsp. olive oil
- 1/4 c. fresh mozzarella to be cut into small cubes
- 1/2 c. grated provolone cheese

Instructions:

1. Set your chicken aside and let it drain for five minutes. Let cool before serving. Preheat the oven to 450 degrees F.

2. Place chicken breasts between two sheets of heavy plastic on a stable, flat surface. (resealable freezer bags work nicely). Pound the chicken until it is 1/2-inch thick with a meat mallet's smooth side.

3. Season chicken liberally with salt and pepper. Using a sifter or strainer, evenly coat both sides of the chicken breasts with flour. Whisk the eggs in a separate bowl and leave aside.

4. Mix 1/2 cup Parmesan cheese with the bread crumbs in a separate bowl and set aside. Set your chicken aside and let it drain for five minutes. Let cool before serving.

5. A flour-coated chicken breast is brushed with beaten eggs. Place the breast in the breadcrumb mixture, pressing crumbs into both sides. Repeat for each breast. Allow the chicken to rest for 10 to 15 minutes.

6. Heat 1/2 inch olive oil in a big skillet over medium-high heat until it shims. Fry the chicken in the hot oil for two minutes on each side or until browned. The chicken will finish cooking in the oven.

7. Set your chicken aside and let it drain for five minutes. Let cool before serving. Season chicken liberally with salt and pepper. Using a sifter or strainer, evenly coat both sides of the chicken breasts with flour.

8. Whisk the eggs in a separate bowl and leave aside. Mix 1/2 cup Parmesan cheese with the bread crumbs in a separate bowl and set aside.

9. A flour-coated chicken breast is brushed with beaten eggs. Place the breast in the breadcrumb mixture, pressing crumbs into both sides. Repeat for each breast. Allow the chicken to rest for 10 to 15 minutes.

10. Heat 1/2 inch olive oil in a big skillet over medium-high heat until it shims. Fry the chicken in the hot oil for two minutes on each side or until browned.

Roast Chicken

A whole chicken is roasted in the oven with herbs and spices.

Ingredients:

- Kosher salt
- 1 (5-6 pound) roasting chicken
- 1 lemon halved
- Freshly ground black pepper
- 1 large bunch of fresh thyme and 20 sprigs
- 1 head of garlic, cut in half crosswise
- Olive oil
- 1 large yellow onion
- 2 tbsp. butter melted
- 4 carrots cut into 2-inch chunks
- 1 bulb of fennel, cut into wedges

Instructions:

1. Preheat the oven to 425 degrees Fahrenheit.
2. Remove the chicken giblets. Rinse the bird from head to toe. Pat the outside dry after removing any excess fat and pin feathers. Season the inside of the chicken well with salt and pepper. Insert the garlic clove, thyme sprig, and two lemon halves into the cavity.
3. Season the skin of the chicken with salt and pepper one more time. Secure the chicken's legs with kitchen twine, then tuck the wing tips beneath the body. Place the fennel, onions, and carrots in a roasting pan.
4. Toss with 20 thyme sprigs, olive oil, salt, and pepper. Place the chicken on top of the mixture evenly distributed throughout the pan.
5. After roasting the bird for 1 1/2 hours, the juices should run clear when you cut between a leg and a thigh. Remove the chicken and veggies from the dish and wrap them in aluminum

foil for about 20 minutes. On a serving plate, arrange the vegetables and cut the chicken.

Pork

Grilled Pork Tenderloin with Peach Salsa

Ingredients:

- 2 pork tenderloins
- 2 ripe peaches, diced
- 1/4 cup chopped red onion
- 1 jalapeño pepper, seeded and minced
- 1/4 cup chopped fresh cilantro
- 2 tbsp lime juice
- 2 tbsp olive oil
- Salt and pepper

Instructions:

1. Preheat a grill to medium-high heat.
2. Brush the pork tenderloins with olive oil and season with salt and pepper.
3. Grill the pork for 5-6 minutes per side, or until it is cooked through.
4. While the pork is grilling, prepare the peach salsa by mixing together the diced peaches, red onion, jalapeño pepper, cilantro, lime juice, olive oil, salt, and pepper in a bowl.
5. Let the pork rest for a few minutes before slicing it thinly against the grain.
6. Serve the grilled pork with the peach salsa spooned over the top.

Slow Cooker Pulled Pork

Ingredients:

- 3 lbs boneless pork shoulder roast
- 1 cup BBQ sauce
- 1/2 cup apple cider vinegar

- 1/4 cup brown sugar
- 1 tbsp smoked paprika
- 1 tbsp garlic powder
- Salt and pepper

Instructions:

1. Season the pork shoulder roast with salt, pepper, smoked paprika, and garlic powder.
2. Place the pork in a slow cooker.
3. In a small bowl, mix together the BBQ sauce, apple cider vinegar, and brown sugar. Pour the mixture over the pork.
4. Cover the slow cooker and cook on low for 8 hours or on high for 4 hours, or until the pork is tender and falls apart easily.
5. Remove the pork from the slow cooker and shred it using two forks.
6. Pour the sauce from the slow cooker over the shredded pork and stir to combine.
7. Serve the pulled pork on buns or rolls, with additional BBQ sauce on the side if desired.

Pork Chops with Apples and Onions

Ingredients:

- 4 bone-in pork chops
- 2 apples, sliced
- 1 yellow onion, sliced
- 2 tbsp olive oil
- 2 tbsp butter
- 1 tbsp brown sugar
- 1 tbsp apple cider vinegar
- Salt and pepper

Instructions:

1. Preheat the oven to 375°F.
2. Heat the olive oil in a large oven-safe skillet over medium-high heat. Season the pork chops with salt and pepper and add them to the skillet. Cook for 4-5 minutes per side, or until they are browned.
3. Remove the pork chops from the skillet and set aside.
4. Add the apples, onion, butter, brown sugar, apple cider vinegar, and a pinch of salt and pepper to the skillet. Cook for a few minutes until the apples and onions are tender.
5. Return the pork chops to the skillet and spoon the apple and onion mixture over the top.
6. Transfer the skillet to the oven and bake for 10-15 minutes, or until the pork chops are cooked through.
7. Let the pork chops rest for a few minutes before serving.

Pork Stir-Fry with Vegetables

Ingredients:

- 1 lb pork loin, cut into strips
- 1 red bell pepper, sliced
- 1 yellow onion, sliced
- 2 cups broccoli florets
- 3 cloves garlic, minced
- 2 tbsp soy sauce
- 1 tbsp cornstarch
- 1 tbsp vegetable oil

Instructions:

1. In a small bowl, mix together the soy sauce and cornstarch to make a sauce.
2. Heat the oil in a large skillet over medium-high heat. Add the

pork and cook until browned on all sides.

3. Add the garlic, red bell pepper, onion, and broccoli to the skillet and cook for a few minutes until the vegetables are tender-crisp.
4. Pour the sauce over the pork and vegetables and stir to combine.
5. Cook for another minute or until the sauce thickens.
6. Serve the stir-fry over rice or noodles.

Grilled Pork Chops with Pineapple Salsa

Ingredients:

- 4 bone-in pork chops
- 1 small pineapple, peeled and diced
- 1/2 red onion, diced
- 1 jalapeño pepper, seeded and minced
- 1/4 cup chopped fresh cilantro
- 2 tbsp lime juice
- 2 tbsp olive oil
- Salt and pepper

Instructions:

1. Preheat a grill to medium-high heat.
2. Brush the pork chops with olive oil and season with salt and pepper.
3. Grill the pork for 4-5 minutes per side, or until it is cooked through.
4. While the pork is grilling, prepare the pineapple salsa by mixing together the diced pineapple, red onion, jalapeño pepper, cilantro, lime juice, olive oil, salt, and pepper in a bowl.
5. Let the pork rest for a few minutes before serving it with the

pineapple salsa spooned over the top.

Slow Cooker Pork Carnitas

Ingredients:

- 3 lbs pork shoulder, cut into large chunks
- 1 onion, chopped
- 3 cloves garlic, minced
- 1/4 cup orange juice
- 1/4 cup lime juice
- 2 tsp ground cumin
- 2 tsp smoked paprika
- Salt and pepper

Instructions:

1. Season the pork shoulder with salt, pepper, cumin, and smoked paprika.
2. Place the pork in a slow cooker and add the onion, garlic, orange juice, and lime juice.
3. Cover the slow cooker and cook on low for 8 hours or on high for 4 hours, or until the pork is tender and falls apart easily.
4. Remove the pork from the slow cooker and shred it using two forks.
5. Heat a large skillet over high heat. Add the shredded pork to the skillet and cook for a few minutes, stirring occasionally, until it is crispy and browned on the outside.
6. Serve the pork carnitas in tacos, burritos, or over rice, with your choice of toppings such as avocado, salsa, cilantro, and lime wedges.

Pork Chops

Pork chops are grilled or pan-fried until cooked through.

Cook Time: 1 hour | Servings: 2

Ingredients:

- 1/2 c. pancetta
- 4 tbsp. (around 60g) of butter, cut into 8 portions
- Two thick pork chops
- 1 skillet

Instructions:

1. To begin, preheat your oven to 450°F (230°C). While the oven is heating up, put crisp half-diced pancetta in a frying pan. Remove from the heat and set aside to cool sufficiently to handle. Wait until you've washed the skillet.
2. Using a very sharp knife, cut a "pocket" along the length of each pork chop. Following that, the pocket will be filled with pancetta. Allow at least 14 inches on the backside and either end of the chop.
3. Stuff the pocket with the cooked pancetta and two butter pads. Place each chop in the same frying pan used to crisp the pancetta.
4. Arrange the extra uncooked pancetta around the chops and fry in the remaining butter.
5. Carefully place everything in the oven.
6. After 45 minutes, remove the pan from the oven and pour the excess grease into a container for later use.
7. Return the meat to the hot oven for 10 minutes to increase color.
8. Serve and enjoy.

Pork Ribs

Pork ribs are slow-cooked with BBQ sauce until tender. These delicious baby back ribs will satisfy everyone in the family. You may be as strict a carnivore as you like with the spices.

Ingredients:

- 1 tbsp. paprika
- 2 tbsp. kosher salt
- 1 tbsp. chili powder
- 1 rack of baby back pork ribs
- 1 1/2 tsp. cayenne pepper
- 1 c. beef broth
- 2 tsp. garlic powder
- 1 tsp. ground black pepper
- 1/4 c. barbeque sauce, or as needed

Instructions:

1. Combine salt, chili powder, paprika, garlic powder, cayenne pepper, and black pepper in a small bowl for the spice rub.
2. Cut the rack of ribs into four equal pieces. Apply spice rub to the whole surface of each piece.
3. Pour the broth into a multifunctional pressure cooker.
4. Cut the ribs into a teepee shape. Close the lid to secure it. Set the timer for 30 minutes and use high pressure according to the manufacturer's instructions. Allow 10 to 15 minutes for the pressure to build.
5. Preheat the oven to 425 degrees F. Cover a baking sheet with aluminum foil.
6. Following the manufacturer's instructions, use the quick-release technique to slowly relieve the pressure, which should take around 5 minutes. The lock and lid have been removed. Transfer the ribs to the baking sheet with tongs. The ribs should be slathered in BBQ sauce all over.
7. Bake in a preheated oven for 7 minutes. Turn the ribs over

after 7 minutes and continue roasting until the meat easily separates from the bone. An instant-read thermometer should read 145 degrees Fahrenheit inside the house. (63 degrees C).

Ham

A cured and roasted leg of a pig that is commonly served on holidays. It's a one-pot keto dinner that takes around 30 minutes to prepare.

Ingredients:

- 2 c. bone broth (or regular broth)
- 2 c. cheddar cheese, grated (save 1/2 cup for garnish)
- 2 oz. cream cheese cut into small pieces
- 10-12 oz. cubed cooked ham
- Salt and Pepper to taste, depending on your broth
- 1 c. Carnivore Noodles (optional)
- 1/2 c. heavy cream
- 1/4 c. bacon crumbles

Instructions:

1. In a thick medium soup, heat the broth until it almost reaches a simmer. Keep the broth on low heat.
2. Whisk the cream cheese cubes into the soup, then mix until all lumps are gone.
3. Stir in the grated cheese, 1/2 cup at a time, until it melts into the mixture.
4. Cubed ham and noodles should be added and cooked through on low heat.
5. Simmer for a further minute on low heat after gently adding heavy cream.
6. Divide the mixture into four big bowls, then top with grated cheddar cheese and saved bacon or bacon crumbles.

Notes:

- Making this soup with items you already have is a wonderful idea.
- You can make this ahead of time by cutting leftover ham or pork roast.
- You can use this recipe to make bone broth or any carton of beef broth you have on hand.

Bacon

Strips of pork belly that are cured and fried until crispy.

Total Time: 1hr | Number of Servings: 3

Ingredients:

- Spring onions
- 500 g. pork belly
- 1 tbsp. Kosher salt for the meat
- 1/4 tsp. black pepper
- 1 tsp. soy sauce
- 1/2 tsp. ground ginger
- 1/2 tsp. olive oil
- Freshly chopped cilantro

Instructions:

1. Make as many holes in the pig's skin as possible without penetrating the meat with a metal skewer.
2. Using a sharp knife, cut the skin into 1-inch strips.
3. Combine water, salt, spring onions, ginger, and black pepper in a large pot. Cook for at least 40 to 60 minutes on medium heat after adding the pork belly meat.
4. When all the water has been drained, place the pig meat on a surface covered with paper towels to air dry. After that, cut it

into bite-sized strips.

5. Fry pork belly with soy sauce in a hot skillet with oil until it is as crisp as you like.

6. For a different flavor, add more spices or Chinese cooking wine here.

7. Serve your crispy, fried pork belly immediately with your favorite side dish after garnishing it with fresh cilantro.

Sausages

Ground pork is seasoned and formed into links, then grilled or fried.

Total Time: 2 hours | Servings: 20

Ingredients:

- 40 g. kosher salt
- 1/4 c. sherry vinegar
- 4 lb. pork shoulder
- 1 lb. pork fat
- 6 g. cracked black pepper
- 35 g. sugar
- 1 c. minced fresh parsley
- 3/4 c. dry sherry
- 20 g. toasted fennel seeds
- 4 g. ground nutmeg
- 1 head of garlic, peeled and chopped

Special Equipment:

- Kitchen scale
- Hog casings
- Meat grinder having coarse and fine dies
- Sausage stuffer

Instructions:

1. Before you begin, ensure all your ingredients are ready, and the meat and fat are very cold (you can put your meat and fat in the freezer for 2 hours). Place the bowls and grinder in the freezer or refrigerator for an hour before using them.

2. Cut the fat and meat into small pieces and refrigerate in an ice-filled bowl. On top of a large bowl of prepared ice, place a medium metal bowl. Cut the meat and fat into an inch to two inches-wide pieces. Fat should be cut somewhat finer than meat.

3. To keep your components cold, place the sliced beef and fat in a bowl in a larger basin filled with ice. Combine the meat and fat as soon as they are sliced. Refrigerate after adding the majority of the spices.

4. Pour in the bulk of your spices and blend quickly. After adding the salt and sugar, repeat the mixing procedure.

5. Place the sausage mixture in the freezer for at least 30 minutes and no more than an hour, either in a closed container or wrapped in plastic wrap.

6. Because sherry is not commonly used in Italian sausage, mix the dry sherry and sherry vinegar before chilling. You can use white wine and white wine vinegar if you like.

7. If you intend to stuff your sausage, take some casings (15 to 18 feet for a batch of 5pound links) and soak them in warm water. You can skip this step if you don't want to stuff your sausage.

8. Set up the grinder. Use the coarse die for Italian sausage, although either would work. Avoid using a very fine die because the meat must be crushed coarsely first, then refrozen, and then processed again with the fine die. Furthermore, Italian sausage is intended to be unpolished.

9. Chill the sausage mixture once it has been ground. Push the sausage mixture through the grinder as quickly as possible. Make sure the ground beef is placed in a cold basin.

10. After you've ground all of the beef, place it in the freezer and clean up the area and grinder. After removing the mixture, add the remaining spices and sherry vinegar combination.

11. Using a stand mixer's paddle attachment, a large wooden spoon, or your clean hands, thoroughly combine the sausage. Allow 90 seconds on level 1 of a stand mixer. Using your hands or a spoon may take a little longer. Like when you knead bread, you want the mixture to become sticky and begin to adhere to itself.

12. The sausage will be ready after it is completed. To cook, take a scoop and roll it into a ball using your hands. Spread your wings a little. Cook for 5 to 10 minutes on each side in a pan over medium-low heat or until browned and done.

☆ ☆ ☆ ☆ ☆

Beef

Grilled Steak with Roasted Vegetables

Ingredients:

- 2 steaks (preferably ribeye or sirloin)
- 2 tbsp olive oil
- 1 tbsp balsamic vinegar
- Salt and black pepper
- 1 red onion, sliced
- 1 red bell pepper, sliced
- 1 zucchini, sliced
- 1 tbsp chopped fresh rosemary
- 1 garlic clove, minced

Instructions:

1. Preheat grill to medium-high heat.
2. In a small bowl, mix olive oil, balsamic vinegar, salt, and black pepper. Brush the steaks with the mixture and set aside.
3. In a large bowl, toss onion, red bell pepper, zucchini, rosemary, garlic, and salt and black pepper to taste.
4. Place vegetables on the grill in a single layer and cook until tender and slightly charred, flipping occasionally, for about 10-12 minutes.
5. Grill the steaks to your desired doneness, flipping once, for about 6-8 minutes per side for medium-rare.
6. Let the steaks rest for 5-10 minutes before slicing. Serve with the roasted vegetables.

Spicy Meatballs with Tomato Sauce

Ingredients:

- 1 lb ground beef
- 1/2 cup breadcrumbs

- 1 egg
- 2 tbsp chopped fresh parsley
- 1 tbsp chopped fresh basil
- 1 garlic clove, minced
- 1/2 tsp salt
- 1/4 tsp black pepper
- 2 tbsp olive oil
- 1 onion, chopped
- 2 garlic cloves, minced
- 1 can (28 oz) crushed tomatoes
- 1 tsp dried oregano
- 1/4 tsp red pepper flakes
- Salt and black pepper

Instructions:

1. Preheat oven to 375°F (190°C).
2. In a large bowl, mix ground beef, breadcrumbs, egg, parsley, basil, garlic, salt, and black pepper. Roll the mixture into 1-inch balls and place on a baking sheet.
3. Bake meatballs for 20-25 minutes, or until cooked through.
4. Meanwhile, heat olive oil in a large saucepan over medium heat. Add onion and garlic and cook until softened, about 5 minutes.
5. Add crushed tomatoes, oregano, red pepper flakes, salt, and black pepper to the saucepan. Bring to a simmer and cook for 10-15 minutes, until the sauce has thickened slightly.
6. Add the cooked meatballs to the saucepan and stir to coat with the tomato sauce. Serve hot with your choice of side dish, such as steamed vegetables or a salad.

Beef and Broccoli Stir-Fry

Ingredients:

- 1 lb beef sirloin, sliced thinly against the grain
- 2 cups broccoli florets
- 1/2 cup sliced carrots
- 1/4 cup sliced green onions
- 3 cloves garlic, minced
- 2 tbsp soy sauce
- 1 tbsp cornstarch
- 1 tbsp vegetable oil

Instructions:

1. In a small bowl, mix together the soy sauce and cornstarch to make a sauce.
2. Heat the oil in a large skillet over medium-high heat. Add the beef and cook until browned on all sides.
3. Add the garlic, broccoli, and carrots to the skillet and cook for a few minutes until the vegetables are tender-crisp.
4. Pour the sauce over the beef and vegetables and stir to combine.
5. Cook for another minute or until the sauce thickens.
6. Serve the stir-fry over rice or noodles and garnish with sliced green onions.

Grilled Flank Steak with Chimichurri Sauce

Ingredients:

- 1 lb flank steak
- 1/2 cup fresh parsley leaves

- 1/4 cup fresh oregano leaves
- 1/4 cup fresh cilantro leaves
- 2 cloves garlic, minced
- 1/4 cup red wine vinegar
- 1/2 cup olive oil
- Salt and pepper

Instructions:

1. Preheat a grill to medium-high heat.
2. Season the flank steak generously with salt and pepper.
3. In a food processor or blender, combine the parsley, oregano, cilantro, garlic, red wine vinegar, and olive oil. Pulse until well combined.
4. Grill the flank steak for 3-4 minutes per side, or until it reaches your desired level of doneness.
5. Let the steak rest for a few minutes before slicing it thinly against the grain.
6. Serve the steak with the chimichurri sauce drizzled over the top.

Beef and Vegetable Stir-Fry

Ingredients:

- 1 lb beef sirloin, sliced thinly against the grain
- 1 red bell pepper, sliced
- 1 yellow onion, sliced
- 2 cups broccoli florets
- 3 cloves garlic, minced
- 2 tbsp soy sauce
- 1 tbsp cornstarch
- 1 tbsp vegetable oil

Instructions:

1. In a small bowl, mix together the soy sauce and cornstarch to make a sauce.
2. Heat the oil in a large skillet over medium-high heat. Add the beef and cook until browned on all sides.
3. Add the garlic, red bell pepper, onion, and broccoli to the skillet and cook for a few minutes until the vegetables are tender-crisp.
4. Pour the sauce over the beef and vegetables and stir to combine.
5. Cook for another minute or until the sauce thickens.
6. Serve the stir-fry over rice or noodles.

Beef and Mushroom Stroganoff

Ingredients:

- 1 lb beef tenderloin, sliced thinly
- 8 oz mushrooms, sliced
- 1/2 cup chopped onion
- 3 cloves garlic, minced
- 1/4 cup flour
- 2 cups beef broth
- 1/2 cup sour cream
- 2 tbsp olive oil
- Salt and pepper
- Chopped parsley for garnish

Instructions:

1. Heat the olive oil in a large skillet over medium-high heat. Add the beef and cook until browned on all sides. Remove the beef from the skillet and set aside.
2. Add the mushrooms, onion, and garlic to the skillet and cook

for a few minutes until the vegetables are tender.

3. Sprinkle the flour over the vegetables and stir to combine. Cook for another minute or until the flour is lightly browned.
4. Slowly pour the beef broth into the skillet, stirring constantly to prevent lumps from forming.
5. Bring the mixture to a simmer and cook for a few minutes until the sauce thickens.
6. Remove the skillet from the heat and stir in the sour cream. Season with salt and pepper to taste.
7. Return the beef to the skillet and stir to coat it with the sauce.
8. Serve the stroganoff over egg noodles and garnish with chopped parsley.

Grilled Steak with Roasted Vegetables

Ingredients:

- 1 lb beef sirloin steak
- 1 red bell pepper, sliced
- 1 zucchini, sliced
- 1 yellow onion, sliced
- 2 cloves garlic, minced
- 2 tbsp olive oil
- Salt and pepper

Instructions:

1. Preheat a grill to medium-high heat.
2. Toss the sliced vegetables with the minced garlic and olive oil, and season with salt and pepper.
3. Grill the steak for 4-5 minutes per side, or until it reaches your desired level of doneness.
4. While the steak is grilling, roast the vegetables in a 400°F oven for 15-20 minutes, or until they are tender and lightly

browned.

5. Let the steak rest for a few minutes before slicing it thinly against the grain.
6. Serve the steak with the roasted vegetables on the side.

Beef and Vegetable Skewers

Ingredients:

- 1 lb beef tenderloin, cut into cubes
- 1 red onion, cut into wedges
- 1 red bell pepper, cut into chunks
- 1 zucchini, cut into rounds
- 1/4 cup olive oil
- 2 tbsp balsamic vinegar
- 2 cloves garlic, minced
- Salt and pepper

Instructions:

1. Soak wooden skewers in water for 30 minutes to prevent them from burning on the grill.
2. Thread the beef and vegetables onto the skewers in any order you like.
3. In a small bowl, whisk together the olive oil, balsamic vinegar, garlic, salt, and pepper.
4. Brush the skewers with the oil mixture, making sure to coat all sides.
5. Preheat a grill to medium-high heat.
6. Grill the skewers for 8-10 minutes, turning occasionally, or until the beef is cooked to your desired level of doneness.
7. Serve the skewers with a side salad or grilled vegetables.

Hamburgers

Ground beef patties are prepared and grilled or fried. Please use fatty ground beef with no more than 80% lean meat to make excellent and juicy hamburger patties.

Ingredients:

- 1 1/2 tsp. sea salt
- 2 lb. ground beef

Instructions:

1. Bring the ground beef to room temperature. Spread the ground beef on a tray or large chopping board, season with salt, and gently mix. Some people recommend sprinkling salt on hamburger patties shortly before cooking to keep the meat from drying out.
2. Combine the salt and other seasonings before forming them to ensure the burgers are evenly seasoned.
3. Divide the ground beef into 8 equal parts. Each one should be rolled into a ball before being pressed into a burger patty form, or the top of a paper cup can be cut off and used as a mold.
4. Firmly push the ground beef piece into the mold to fill all the gaps. Using the mold, you may make uniform burger patties less likely to crumble when cooking.
5. Melt butter in a griddle pan or nonstick frying pan over medium-high heat. Ensure the pan is hot enough that when water drops on the surface, it evaporates immediately.
6. You can add a tablespoon of fat if you want, but it may not be necessary if you use fatty ground beef. Add two burger patties and keep the pan temperature high to evenly brown the patties.
7. Cook for 3 to 4 minutes. Please do not press down or move the burgers while they are cooking to avoid them from falling apart and achieve the proper level of browning, giving the burgers a great flavor.
8. It is better to handle them as little as possible. Grill for another

3 to 4 minutes for medium-rare or 5 minutes for medium after flipping the burgers using a big spatula. Cook for a few minutes longer if you prefer them well done.

9. Arrange the burgers on a dish and set them aside to rest. They should stay in the fridge for five days but must be consumed within a few days.

The Perfect Grilled Steak

Beef is grilled or pan-fried to the desired doneness.

Ingredients:

- 4 rib-eye steaks about 1 1/2" thick, around 1 pound each
- 1 tsp. salt plus more for seasoning
- Pepper
- 1 tsp. cornstarch

Instructions:

1. In a small bowl, combine the salt and cornstarch. After patting the steaks dry, rub the salt mixture on them.
2. Place the steaks on a wire rack in the freezer for 30 to 1 hour to chill.
3. In the meantime, start a fire on your charcoal grill and clean the grates for steak cooking.
4. Season the steaks with pepper.
5. On the grill, allow 4 to 8 minutes per side.
6. Remove the grill and cover it with foil. Before serving, allow 5 minutes. To serve, slice thinly across the grain at an angle.

Roast Beef and Vegetables

A cut of beef is roasted in the oven until cooked through.

Cook Time: 20 minutes | Servings: 3-4

Ingredients:

- Salt
- Freshly ground pepper
- 2 lb. Top rump of beef, room temperature
- 2 onions, peeled and chopped
- Olive oil for drizzling
- 2 tsp. thyme
- 1 lb. New potatoes, halved
- 1 bulb of garlic, broken into cloves and peeled
- 2 c. beef stock
- 3 carrots, peeled and chopped
- 2 bay leaves
- 2 sticks of celery, roughly chopped

Instructions:

1. Preheat oven to 425 degrees Fahrenheit. (220 C). Season the meat with salt, pepper, and thyme all over with a little olive oil.
2. In a cast iron skillet heated over high heat, sear the beef for 3–4 minutes on each side, turning it occasionally, until it is nicely browned but not scorched.
3. Arrange the vegetables and bay leaves in the bottom of a roasting pan. Drizzle the roast with olive oil and serve.
4. After baking the roast for about 15 minutes, reduce the oven temperature to 375 F. (190 C). Roast for 13-15 minutes for rare, 17-19 minutes for medium, and 22-25 minutes for cooked through.
5. Check the meat with a thermometer to ensure it is at the desired temperature (medium rare is 145°F, and medium is

160°F). While the roast is cooking, baste it a couple of times and watch the vegetables. If they begin to burn, cover the pan with a foil tent.

6. Remove the beef from the oven and set it aside on a board, covered with foil and a kitchen towel, for 15 to 30 minutes. Remember that the meat will continue to cook while resting, so remove it from the oven when it is 5°F below the ideal temperature. If the veggies still need to be cooked while the meat rests, return them to the oven until they are.

Meatloaf

Ground beef is mixed with breadcrumbs, eggs, and spices, then baked in the oven.

Total Time: 1 hour 40 minutes | Servings: 8

Ingredients:

- 3/4 c. milk
- 2 eggs, beaten
- 1 tsp. dry mustard
- 1/4 c. finely chopped onion
- 2 tbsp. packed brown sugar
- 2/3 c. fine dry bread crumbs/2 c. soft bread crumbs
- 2 tbsp. Snipped fresh parsley
- 1/2 tsp. dried leaf sage, basil/oregano, crushed
- 1 tsp. salt
- 1 1/2 lb. lean ground beef, lamb, or pork
- 1/8 tsp. black pepper
- 1/4 c. ketchup

Instructions:

1. Mix eggs and milk in a medium bowl before adding bread

crumbs, onion, parsley, salt, and pepper. Add in the ground beef. Blend gently with clean hands until well combined. Press the mixture gently into an 8x4x2-inch loaf pan.

2. Bake for 1 to 1-1/4 hours at 350°F or until an internal thermometer registers 160°F. After combining ketchup, sugar, and mustard in a bowl, spread over meat. Bake for another 10 minutes. Allow 10 minutes of rest time before cutting into 8 slices.

Tacos

Beef is seasoned and served in a taco shell with toppings like cheese, lettuce, and salsa.

Ingredients:

- 1 tsp. chili powder
- 1 medium onion, chopped
- 1 lb. lean ground beef
- 1/2 tsp. salt
- 8 oz. tomato sauce
- 1/2 tsp. garlic powder
- 1 1/2 c. shredded Cheddar cheese (6 oz)
- 4.6 oz. Old El Paso Crunchy Taco Shells (12 Count)
- 2 c. shredded lettuce
- 3/4 c. Old El Paso Thick 'n Chunky salsa
- 2 medium tomatoes, chopped
- 3/4 c. sour cream, if needed

Instructions:

1. Set the oven temperature to 250°F. Brown the ground beef and onion in a large skillet, constantly stirring, for 8 to 10 minutes or until thoroughly cooked.

2. Season with salt, garlic powder, and chili powder. Reduce the

heat to low, cover the pot, and let it simmer for 10 minutes.

3. Place the taco shells on an ungreased cookie sheet. Cook for 5 minutes at 250°F.

4. Layer the meat mixture, cheese, lettuce, and tomatoes in each taco shell to build the tacos.

5. Serve topped with salsa and sour cream.

Lamb

Grilled Lamb Chops

Lamb chops are marinated and then grilled until cooked through.

Cook Time: 12 minutes | Servings: 4

Ingredients:

- 1 tbsp. chopped fresh thyme leaves, and 1 large sprig
- 8 lamb loin or rib chops
- 1 tsp. freshly squeezed lemon juice
- 1/4 tsp. freshly ground black pepper
- 1/2 c. dry white wine or low-sodium chicken broth
- 4 tbsp. unsalted butter, divided
- 1 large garlic clove smashed
- 3/4 tsp. kosher salt, divided
- 1 small shallot, finely chopped
- 1 tbsp. Finely grated lemon zest

Instructions:

1. Season the lamb. After taking the lamb chops from the fridge, season with 1/2 teaspoon salt, 1/2 teaspoon pepper, and 1/2 teaspoon chopped thyme. Allow the lamb chops to come to room temperature for 5 minutes.

2. Get the lamb ready. Melt 2 tablespoons butter in a 12-inch skillet over medium-high heat. Cook for 4 to 6 minutes, or up to 10 minutes if using thicker lamb chops, or until a rich, brown crust forms on the bottom.

3. Change the lamb. Cook for another 4 to 6 minutes or until an instant-read thermometer inserted into the center of the lamb chops reads 145°F.

4. Arrange on a plate. Wrap the lamb chops in foil and place them on a plate. Pour away everything except 2 tablespoons of the rendered fat.

5. Sauté the thyme, shallot, and garlic in a skillet. The heat should be reduced to medium. Sauté the shallot, garlic, and

thyme sprig for about a minute or until the onion softens and browns.

6. Deglaze the pan. Before deglazing with the wine, broth, and lemon juice, scrape any burnt bits off the pan's bottom.

7. Finish the sauce. Cook for 1 to 2 minutes or until the liquid has been reduced by half. Combine the remaining 1/4 teaspoon salt, 2 tablespoons butter, and lemon zest in a mixing bowl. Simmer for about a minute or until the butter melts and the sauce thickens slightly. Taste and season with salt and pepper as needed. After pouring the sauce over the lamb chops, serve immediately.

Notes:

- Lamb chops can be prepared by seasoning them with salt, pepper, thyme, and lemon zest and chilling them for up to an hour.
- Lamb chops can be stored for about 3 days. Keep leftovers in an airtight container in the refrigerator.

Carnivore Lamb Leg Roast

A leg of lamb is roasted in the oven with herbs and spices.

Ingredients:

- 1 tsp. salt
- 3 1/2 lb. leg of lamb
- 1 tbsp. chopped fresh rosemary
- 2 tabs of melted fat or bacon grease
- 4 minced garlic cloves
- 1 tsp. pepper
- 1 tbsp. Chopped fresh thyme leaves

Instructions:

1. Allow the lamb to come to room temperature on the kitchen

counter for two to three hours. You can ensure uniform cooking by doing so. The oven is preheated at 375°F (190°C).

2. In a small bowl, combine all of your chosen seasonings. Place the lamb in a roasting pan. Before pressing the spice mixture into the top side of the lamb, score it all over with a sharp knife. Alternately, make around 15 small slits all over the top of the lamb with a paring knife and insert seasonings into the incisions.

3. Roast the lamb for 30 minutes, fat side up, to brown and sear the outside. Once seared, remove and cover with foil, then put back in the oven.

4. Continue to roast for 45 minutes at 250°F (120°C). Transfer the lamb to a dish and set it aside for 15 minutes before slicing. Keep the fat and liquid in the roasting dish.

5. Using a large, sharp knife, slice the lamb roast while holding it steady on a carving fork. Always cut with the grain. Drizzle the fat and juice on top before serving.

6. The rare to medium-rare meat obtained by this approach tastes the best. Internal temperatures for rare and medium meats should be around 135°F (58°C) and 150°F (65°C), respectively.

Lamb Kofta

Ground lamb is spiced and shaped into meatballs or sausage-like shapes before being cooked. Lamb kofta is a Middle Eastern dish made of ground lamb, onion, garlic, and numerous spices shaped into patties, balls, or logs and grilled. The meal is commonly served skewered (kabob style) and unskewered, depending on the cooking process and option.

Ingredients:

- 1/2 tsp. salt
- 1 medium Spanish onion, minced

- 1 lb. lean ground lamb
- 1/4 c. finely chopped curly parsley
- 1 clove of garlic, minced
- 1/4 tsp. ground pepper
- 1/4 tsp. allspice
- 1/4 tsp. Cinnamon
- 1/8 tsp. ground cloves

Instructions:

1. Preheat the grill to medium-high heat. In a medium mixing bowl, knead the lamb with the onion, garlic, parsley, salt, pepper, cinnamon, allspice, and cloves until the ingredients are evenly distributed.
2. Divide the mixture into four equal pieces. Form each component into an 8-inch sausage. The meat is impaled on a strong metal skewer.
3. Lightly oil a folded paper towel. Hold the towel with tongs. Dredge the grill rack along the grates in your direction to grease it because the oil will soon cook off. You should do this straight away before adding the meat.
4. After 9 to 13 minutes of cooking time, flip the lamb kofta every 3 to 4 minutes. Allow the skewer to rest on a cutting surface for 4 minutes before slicing.

Notes:

- Flare-ups on the grill are probable if your lamb is not exceptionally lean. If this happens while grilling kofta on a gas grill, switch off one of the burners and set the skewers over the side of the grill that has been turned off.
- To prevent sticking, lubricate the grill.

Lamb Curry

Cubes of lamb are simmered in a spicy sauce.

Total Time: 1 hour 35 minutes

Ingredients:

- 500 g. Lamb
- 2 onions
- 1 tsp. Chili Powder
- 50 ml. Olive Oil
- 1 tsp. Ginger Paste
- 3 tomatoes
- 1 tsp. salt
- 1 tsp. garlic Paste
- 1 tsp. turmeric Powder Haldi
- 1 tsp. coriander Powder
- 1/2 tsp. gram Masala
- 500 ml. Water
- 1 tsp. dried Fenugreek Leaves Methi
- Coriander

Instructions:

1. Heat the olive oil in a skillet over medium heat until hot. Cook for 5 minutes or until the onions are soft.
2. Cook for 1 minute after adding the ginger and garlic paste. Cook for 5 minutes or until the tomatoes are soft.
3. Add salt, turmeric powder, chili powder, and coriander powder, and simmer the spices for 3-4 minutes.
4. Add water and simmer for 8 to 10 minutes after adding the spices to the lamb or mutton.
5. If the meat is still not done, add more water to help it cook for another 45 to 60 minutes.
6. To keep the meat from burning, cover the pan with a lid.
7. Stir in the coriander, fenugreek, and gram masala. Enjoy!

Lamb Shank

A lamb shank is slow-cooked in a flavorful broth until tender.

Total Time: 3 hours 30 minutes

Ingredients:

- 1 tbsp. olive oil
- 4 lamb shanks
- 1 c. carrot, finely diced
- 1 onion finely diced
- 1/3 c. balsamic vinegar
- 4 cloves garlic minced
- 1 c. finely diced celery
- 2 bay leaves
- 3 tbsp. tomato paste
- 1/4 tsp. pepper
- 3 c. beef stock
- 1/4 tsp. salt
- 1 tsp. dried thyme

Instructions:

1. Preheat the oven to 350 degrees F. (175 degrees Celsius).
2. Season the lamb shank on all sides with salt and pepper. Sear the shanks on all sides in a large pan with oil over medium-high heat (approx. 8 minutes). After searing, place on a dish.
3. When the veggies soften, add the garlic, onion, celery, and carrot, and cook for 5 minutes.
4. After adding the balsamic vinegar, tomato paste, beef stock, thyme, bay leaves, salt, and pepper, stir everything together in the pan. Bring to a gentle boil. When the sauce has finished simmering, return the lamb shanks to the pan and spoon some

sauce. Cook for 1 1/2 hours in the oven with a cover on.

☆ ☆ ☆ ☆ ☆

Seafood

Fried Shrimp

Whole shrimp are breaded and fried in hot oil until golden brown.

Prep Time: 15 minutes | Total Time: 19 minutes | Servings: 5

Ingredients:

- 1/2 c. flour
- 1 lb. shrimp peeled and deveined
- 1 tsp. onion powder
- 2 c. oil
- 1 tsp. paprika
- 1 tsp. garlic powder
- 1/2 tsp. salt
- 2 eggs, beaten
- 1/2 tsp. black pepper
- 1 c. panko breadcrumbs

Instructions:

1. Toss the shrimp with the salt and pepper in a medium bowl.
2. Add the flour, onion powder, garlic powder, paprika, salt, and pepper in a small bowl.
3. Place panko in a third bowl and eggs in a second.
4. Coat the shrimp in the flour mixture, the egg, and the panko crumbs. Arrange them on a tray or a flat dish.
5. The oil temperature in a deep skillet or deep frying pan should be around 375 degrees Fahrenheit. (190 degrees C).
6. Cook a few shrimp at a time in the hot oil until golden brown. 2 to 3 minutes, depending on the size of the shrimp.
7. Using a slotted spoon, remove the fried shrimp and place them on paper towels to drain.

Notes:

- Cook the shrimp in batches to avoid overcrowding the pot.
- As the coating thickens, it becomes crisper.

- Be careful not to overcook them. When overcooked, they become chewy and difficult to consume.

Lobster with Butter

A whole lobster is boiled and then served with melted butter.

Total Time: 25 minutes

Ingredients:

- 2 tbsp. water
- 1 3/4 lb. live lobster or 2 uncooked lobster tails
- 2 tomatoes cut into large chunks
- 1 clove of garlic, very finely minced
- 1/2 c. salted butter 1 stick, cut into 1 tablespoon chunks
- A few fresh basils leave chiffonade

Instructions:

Using Lobster Tails:

1. Cut the lobster's shell down its back using sharp kitchen shears. Turn the bottom shell over and chop it down. Remove the meat by peeling off the shell.

Using Whole Lobster:

1. Bring a large pot of water to a boil if you intend to use live, whole lobster. Turn off the heat and add the lobster. Cook with the cover on for three minutes. After removing the lobster meat from the shell, cut it into large chunks.
2. 1 tablespoon of water should be simmering on low heat in a saucepan. Add 1 tsp of butter and whisk. After the first batch of butter has melted, add more. Continue by adding each remaining piece of butter one at a time. Make sure the mixture does not boil to prevent the butter from separating.

3. Add the lobster pieces and simmer for 5 minutes on medium-low heat, turning about once per minute. Make sure the mixture does not boil. After extracting the lobster, divide it into two serving basins.

4. Add the garlic and raise the heat slightly in the same saucepan with the remaining butter. When the mixture smells good, add the tomatoes and cook for a few minutes or until some juices are released. Lightly smash the tomatoes to extract more juice. Then finish with the basil. Serve immediately with tomatoes on top of the lobster.

Grilled Fish

A piece of fish is marinated and then grilled until cooked through.

Ingredients:

- 1 tbsp. olive oil
- 3 slices of lemon
- 1 whole fish, gutted and scaled
- 1–2 tsp. kosher salt
- 1 small bunch of fresh parsley
- Spray oil

Instructions:

1. Prepare a grill with off-center coals for two-zone grilling. As a result, a hot and cool zone for cooking is formed. Around 400 °F should be considered hot.

2. Pat the fish dry from the cavity to the skin with a paper towel. Fill the cavity with lemon and parsley after applying salt.

3. Drizzle the olive oil over the outside of the fish, coating both sides completely. Season both sides liberally with salt.

4. Spray some oil on the hot side of the grill grates, but not too close. Place the fish onto the greased grates over the hot

embers to sear and crisp the skin.

5. You will now turn the fish over while it is still cooking. Spray a separate section of the grates over the hot coals where you want to flip the fish, then use a fish spatula or stiff spatula to carefully flip it over. Cook for 2 minutes.

6. If your fish becomes excessively browned, move it to the intermediate region (halfway between the hot and cool zones) to cook it more slowly.

7. If you haven't achieved the desired char/color on the outside, repeat the high-heat searing process of spraying and flipping; this time, add spray oil to the fish's surface. Spray directly into the skin that is facing up just before flipping.

8. Once the fish has reached an acceptable color, move the fish to the indirect side to finish cooking. Spray the grill grates where you intend to move the fish with nonstick cooking spray.

9. Keep an eye on the meat as it changes from transparent to opaque to determine when the fish is done. The fish is done for a more precise reading when a thermometer reads 140 degrees.

10. When finished, serve immediately, and don't forget to appreciate that succulent cheek meat bite!

Seafood Paella

A traditional Spanish dish made with rice, seafood, and vegetables.

Total Time: 65 minutes | Servings: 6 servings

Ingredients:

- 1/4 tsp. salt
- 4 1/2 c. chicken stock
- 1/2 yellow onion

- 3 tbsp. olive oil
- 1/2 tsp. saffron threads
- 1/2 red bell pepper
- 6 oz. mild dried chorizo sausage
- 14 oz. fire-roasted diced tomatoes
- 3 cloves garlic
- 3 c. short-grain rice
- 1 lb. large shrimp
- 1 lb. littleneck clams,
- 1 c. frozen green peas
- 1 lb. mussels
- 1/4 c. chopped parsley

Instructions:

1. Light a charcoal grill and let it burn until it is completely covered in gray ash (375°F for gas grills).
2. Bring the stock to a boil in a saucepan over medium heat to steep the saffron. Season with salt and saffron. Allow the saffron to steep for at least 15 minutes after turning off the heat. Taste and season with more salt if necessary.
3. Heat the oil in a 12- to 14-inch cast iron or stainless steel skillet over medium heat to prepare the soffit foundation. After adding the red pepper, cook for 5 to 7 minutes or until the onion is translucent. Stir in the chorizo and garlic.
4. Arrange the items near the grill. Place the pan with the sofrito, rice, tomatoes, infused stock, salt, peas, shrimp, mussels, and clams near the grill.
5. Place the skillet with the sofrito on the grill to cook the paella. Toss the rice often for 4 to 5 minutes or until gently toasted and coated with oil.
6. After mixing, add the stock, tomatoes, and peas. After seasoning, add more salt if desired.
7. Spread the rice evenly across the bottom of the pan. Cook the rice on the grill without stirring for 15 minutes or until the rice

has absorbed the majority of the liquid. If the mixture appears dry without stirring, add about 1 cup of hot water.

8. Place the mussels and clams in the rice, hinge sides up, to allow the shell juices to seep into the rice. Form a circle with the shrimp and shellfish.

9. Cook the dish for another 6 to 10 minutes, depending on how hot your grill is, or until the mussels and clams are open and the rice is well cooked.

Clam Chowder

A creamy soup made with clams, potatoes, and onions.

Ingredients:

- 1 tsp. minced garlic
- 1 1/2 tsp. kosher salt
- Chopped parsley to garnish
- 4 slices bacon, chopped
- 1/2 c, chopped onion
- 2 tbsp. butter
- 8 oz. bottle of clam juice
- 1/4 tsp. ground black pepper
- 3 c. peeled and chopped celery root
- 16 oz. raw chopped clams
- 8 oz. mascarpone cheese
- 1 1/2 c. water

Instructions:

1. Cook the bacon in a large saucepan over medium heat for 2 to 3 minutes or until it is lightly browned but not crispy.

2. Cook for 2 to 3 minutes until the onions are translucent and fragrant, with the celery root, onion, garlic, salt, and pepper.

3. Cover and cook on low heat for 15 to 20 minutes when the

celery root is tender. Pour in the water and clam juice.

4. When you add the clams and stir, the mascarpone cheese should melt, and the broth should become creamy.
5. Simmer on low for 3 minutes or until the clams are slightly cooked. Never, ever boil.
6. Remove from the heat and stir in the butter, allowing it to melt.
7. Taste and add extra salt and pepper as needed.
8. Garnish with parsley and serve hot.

Game

Grilled Rabbit

A whole rabbit is marinated and grilled until fully cooked. This recipe is intended to be cooked on the grill because the flavor is fantastic, but it also roasts well at 200°C/400°F/gas. If you're cooking the rabbit pieces in the oven, turn them several times to ensure even coloring and cooking. If you want to cook it on the grill, you'll need five wooden or metal skewers.

Here are some general guidelines for roasting or grilling:

- Liver and Kidneys: 4 minutes
- Shoulder and Legs: 35-40 minutes
- Ribs and Saddle: 15-20 minutes
- Belly: 25-30 minutes

Ingredients:

- 4 cloves garlic peeled
- 1.2 kg rabbit, preferably wild, jointed
- 1 lemon, zest, and juice of
- Olive oil
- 1 tsp. honey
- 1 handful of fresh thyme and rosemary leaves picked
- 4 thick slices of higher-welfare pancetta
- Salt
- Freshly ground black pepper

Instructions:

1. Place the rabbit bits in a bowl. Using a mortar and pestle or a liquidizer, crush or blend the thyme and rosemary leaves to a pulp. Then, repeat the process with the garlic cloves. After mixing in 8 tablespoons of olive oil, lemon zest, juice, and honey, pour this over the rabbit. Set the meat aside to come to room temperature while you start the grill.
2. Gather a few fresh thyme sprigs and tie them together to make a small brush. Each time you turn the meat, dab a little

marinade onto it to create a flavor-coated layer.

3. Remove the meat from the marinade, season with salt and pepper, and set aside. Assemble the pancetta between the two pieces of the belly with three skewers. Preheat the grill for the shoulders and legs. After they've been cooking for 10 minutes, add the belly. After another ten minutes, add the saddle and ribs. Make sure to flip the meat over from time to time.

4. Maintain the temperature by basting it with the marinade regularly. Each kidney should be divided in half and opened like a book. 1 piece of liver (cut into four pieces), 1 kidney, and more liver should be on each remaining skewer.

5. When the meat is perfectly cooked, add the skewered chunks of kidney and liver to the grill and cook until golden, together with the two remaining slices of pancetta. After a few minutes, place the browned pancetta on top of the meat toward the cooler end of the grill. Gather everyone around the table now.

6. Serve the rabbit with white beans, roast potatoes, grilled vegetables, or salads, depending on your mood and the weather. Simply place the meat on a board and serve.

Venison Stew

Venison stew includes slices of venison simmered in a tomato and spice-based sauce until tender.

Ingredients:

- 1/4 c. all-purpose flour
- 2 lb. venison stew meat (or moose, elk, beef, antelope, bear – any red meat)
- 2 tsp. salt, divided
- 1–2 tbsp. high heat-tolerant oil or fat (deer/ duck/ beef fat, clarified butter avocado oil)

- 1 tsp. pepper
- 3–4 large carrots, diced
- 1 lb. baby, gold potatoes, quartered
- 1 onion, diced
- 3 celery stalks, diced
- 2 tsp. Herbs de Provence
- 4–5 garlic cloves, minced
- 4 c. beef or venison stock
- 1 (15oz.) can of diced tomatoes, drained
- 5–10 dashes of Worcestershire sauce
- 1/2 c. red wine (dry red like a Cabernet or Bordeaux is lovely)

Optional:

- 3 tbsp. corn starch, tapioca starch, or arrowroot powder,

Instructions:

1. Whisk together the flour, 1/2 teaspoon of pepper, and 1 teaspoon of salt in a larger mixing bowl. To remove any liquid, pat the venison dry thoroughly with a towel. Toss the venison chunks in the flour mixture again as soon as they are evenly coated.
2. Heat the oil or fat in a large skillet set over medium-high heat. When the pan is hot, sear the venison all over. Working in batches may be necessary to avoid crowding the meat.
3. After searing the meat and potatoes, place them in the bottom of a slow cooker.
4. Next, combine the tomatoes, stock, wine, Worcestershire sauce, Herbs de Provence, carrots, celery, onion, garlic, and the remaining 1 teaspoon salt and 1/2 teaspoon pepper in a large mixing bowl.
5. Set your slow cooker to low for 8 to 9 hours. Remove a few spoonfuls of the liquid after about 6 hours and pour them into a bowl or cup as an optional step for a thick stew. Stir constantly as the starch is added to form a slurry. After adding

the slurry, thoroughly stir the stew and cover it with a lid to finish cooking.

6. Keep warm and serve with crusty bread!

Notes:

- Cook for 4-5 hours on high, but 8-9 hours on low is preferable. The meat will be softer, and the flavors will blend better.
- Because it's so lovely, seek out Herbs de Provence rather than substituting them.

Roast Duck

A whole duck is roasted in the oven with herbs and spices such as thyme, rosemary, parsley, and lemon.

Total Time: 2 hours 10 minutes | Servings: 4

Ingredients:

- 2 tbsp. olive oil
- 1 tbsp. garlic powder
- 5 lb. duck
- 1 tsp. Rosemary
- 1 tsp. thyme
- 1 tsp. sea salt
- 6 slices lemon for garnish
- 1 tsp. parsley
- 3 sprigs of fresh thyme and rosemary
- 1/2 lemon, juiced

Instructions:

1. Preheat the oven to 350 degrees Fahrenheit. Clean, dry, and salt the duck. Combine the olive oil, spices, and lemon juice to paste.

2. Spread the paste on the duck. Place the remainder of the squeezed lemon inside the duck's cavity.

3. In a roasting pan, combine the duck and 1/2 cup water.

4. Cook the duck for 120 minutes, basting every 30 minutes. It's done when the duck's fluids are clear and golden brown.

5. Remove from the oven and set aside for ten to fifteen minutes to cool. Serve immediately after slicing. Garnish with lemon slices, pan juices, and fresh thyme or rosemary.

6. Refrigerate in a glass dish for two days.

Pheasant Bake

A whole pheasant is baked in the oven with herbs and spices.

Ingredients:

- 1/4 bunch of rosemary, divided use
- 1 pheasant
- 1/4 bunch of sage, divided use
- 1 bunch of escarole
- 4 cloves of garlic, thinly sliced
- 1/4 lb. white truffle butter melted
- 1 c. duck and veal demi-glace
- 1/4 c. white wine or vermouth
- 10 Cipollini onions peeled

Instructions:

1. Preheat the oven to 400 degrees Fahrenheit. Choose each herb with a single leaf; remove any stems. Half of the herbs should be finely chopped and set aside.

2. Gently detach the pheasant skin from the breasts and thighs with your index finger to avoid tearing the skin. The full-leaf herbs should be applied piece by piece beneath the epidermis.

3. After being coated in softened truffle butter, the bird should

have a shell-like exterior.

4. Season with salt and pepper to taste.

5. Bake the bird for 10 minutes at 400 degrees, then reduce the heat to 350 degrees for another 30 minutes. Place the bird on top of the peeled cipollini onions in a skillet. While the bird roasts, sauté the escarole with the garlic and season with salt and pepper. You may need to add a little water if you want the escarole to be soft.

6. After deglazing the roasting pan with white wine or vermouth, add the demi-glace. Before reducing by half and straining, stir in the minced herbs and season with salt and pepper to taste.

7. Remove the breast meat from the pheasant (three lengthwise slices for each breast), then remove the thighs. Each plate should include a thigh and a layer of sliced breast meat.

8. Serve with chilled white wine and a dollop of sauce on top.

Wild Boar Chops

Wild boar chops are grilled or pan-fried until cooked through.

Total Time: 6 hours 30 minutes | Total Servings: 4

Ingredients:

- 1 tbsp. Lawry's Seasoned Pepper
- 2 tsp Lawry's Seasoned Salt
- 2 lb. boar/pork chops
- 2 tbsp. minced fresh rosemary
- 1/3 cup olive oil
- 8 whole garlic cloves – (to 10)
- 1 lemon, juice only
- 1 c. carrots
- 6 whole peeled shallots – (to 8)
- 1 cup dry red wine

- 2 celery stalks cut 2 " pieces
- 1/2 cup chilled butter cut into 4 pieces

Instructions:

1. Season the meat with Lawry's Seasoned Salt and Lawry's Seasoned Pepper. Seasoned chops are combined with 1/4 cup olive oil, rosemary, and lemon juice. Refrigerate for 6 to 12 hours, covered.

2. Heat the remaining oil in a large oven-safe skillet. Chops are added and lightly browned on both sides. Remove and set aside the chops.

3. Sauté the carrots, celery, garlic, and shallots until they brown.

4. Return the chops to the pan and preheat the oven to 375°F. Cook for 5 to 8 minutes more or until the chops are done and the shallots are tender.

5. Keep the chops warm after removing them from the pan. Place the pan over medium-high heat and add the wine. Reduce the wine to about 2 teaspoons. After removing from the heat, whisk in the chilled butter until melted.

6. Arrange the chops on top of the vegetables on serving plates. Serve the sauce over the chops.

☆ ☆ ☆ ☆ ☆

Snacks and Salads

French Fries

Potatoes are sliced and fried in hot oil until crispy.

Total Time: 30 minutes | Servings: 4

Ingredients:

- 1/3 c. white sugar
- 2 c. warm water
- 6 c. vegetable oil for frying
- 2 large russet potatoes, peeled and sliced into 1/4-inch strips
- Salt to taste

Instructions:

1. Combine the heated water and sugar in a medium mixing bowl. Soak potatoes in a water mixture for 15 minutes. Remove the potatoes from the water and pat them dry with paper towels.
2. In a deep fryer, heat the oil to 375°F (190 degrees C).
3. Cook potatoes in hot oil for 5–6 minutes or until golden. Season with salt and pat dry with paper towels.

Chicken Salad

A salad with cubed chicken, vegetables, and a vintage

Total Time: 20 minutes | Servings: 4 servings

Ingredients:

For the Salad:

- 1 medium tomato, diced
- 1 head of baby romaine lettuce, diced
- 1 1/2 c. diced cucumber
- 1 small red pepper, diced

- 1 1/4 lb. cooked chicken, diced
- 1/4 c. diced red onion
- 1/3 c. Kalamata olives
- 1/2 c. crumbled feta

For the Dressing:

- 1/4 c. red wine vinegar
- 1/4 c. avocado or olive oil
- 2 cloves garlic, minced
- 1 tbsp. lemon juice
- 1/2 tsp. dried marjoram
- 2 tsp. Dijon mustard
- Salt and pepper to taste

Instructions:

For the Salad:

1. Option 1: Arrange all ingredients in decorative lines on a large dish. Allow guests to take as many servings as they like.
2. Option 2: Combine all ingredients in a large mixing bowl and divide them evenly among four large plates.

For the Dressing:

1. Shake all the dressing ingredients thoroughly in a jar or bottle with a sealable top. Serve alongside the salad.

Chicken Salad

A salad with cubed chicken, vegetables, and a vinaigrette dressing.

Ingredients:

- 7 tbsp. reduced-fat balsamic vinaigrette dressing
- 1 lb. uncooked thin sliced chicken breasts
- 1 medium red onion cut into 1/4-inch slices

- 1 medium zucchini (8 oz), cut lengthwise in half
- 6 c. torn arugula
- 4 plum (Roma) tomatoes, cut in half
- 1/2 c. crumbled feta cheese (2 oz)

Instructions:

1. Preheat a gas or charcoal grill. Brush 1 tablespoon of the dressing over the chicken. Brush the grill rack gently. Over medium heat, grill the chicken, zucchini, and onion. Cook, flipping once, for 8 to 10 minutes, or until the chicken is no longer pink in the center and the vegetables are soft. For the last 4 minutes of cooking, grill the tomato halves.
2. Remove the chicken and vegetables from the grill and place them on a cutting board. Cut the chicken into thin crosswise slices, and roughly chop the vegetables.
3. Combine the chicken, vegetables, and the remaining 6 tablespoons of dressing in a large mixing bowl. Combine the arugula and cheese in a mixing bowl. Serve immediately.

Caesar Salad

A salad with romaine lettuce, croutons, Parmesan cheese, and a Caesar dressing.

Total Time: 30 minutes | Servings: 4 to 6

Ingredients:

- 4 cloves of garlic, minced
- 1/2 c. high-quality extra virgin olive oil, including more for brushing
- 1/4 c. fresh lemon juice
- 1 baguette, preferably a day old, thinly sliced
- 4 oz. Parmesan cheese, grated
- 2 large eggs

- 1 tsp. anchovy paste, or 1 to 2 anchovies, minced
- 1/2 tsp. kosher salt (or to taste)
- 4 to 6 small heads of romaine lettuce, rinsed, patted dry, wilted outer leaves discarded
- 1/4 tsp. Freshly ground black pepper (or to taste)

Instructions:

1. Combine 1/2 cup olive oil and garlic in a large mixing bowl. Allow at least 30 minutes for your stay.
2. While the garlic sits, make the croutons. Lay out the baguette slices on a baking sheet. This might have to be done in batches.
3. Brush or spray melted butter with olive oil. If you want garlicky croutons, dip a pastry brush in the garlic-infused oil you made in the previous step.
4. Broil the tops for 1-2 minutes or until lightly browned. Don't walk away because these can quickly turn brown to charred. Set aside to cool after removing from the oven.
5. To the oil-garlic mixture, add the minced anchovies or anchovy paste, as well as the eggs. Whisk until completely smooth. Squeeze in 1/4 cup lemon juice after seasoning with salt and pepper. Half of the Parmesan cheese should be included. Season with additional lemon juice, salt, and pepper to taste. The lemon should give the dressing a tang without overpowering it.
6. Remove romaine lettuce chunks with your hands: Remove romaine lettuce chunks with your hands rather than with a knife. Toss the salad in the dressing until evenly coated. Toss with the rest of the Parmesan cheese.
7. To serve, coarsely chop the toasted bread and toss it with the salad. Brush in any crumbs left over from the bread-chopping process. Toss and serve immediately.

Steak Salad

A salad with grilled steak, vegetables, and a vinaigrette dressing.

Total Time: 45 minutes | Servings: 4 servings

Ingredients:

- 1/4 c. balsamic vinegar
- 1/2 tsp. kosher salt
- 1/4 tsp. black pepper
- 2 tsp. Dijon mustard
- 1/2 c. extra-virgin olive oil
- 1 tsp. mayonnaise, optional
- Kosher salt for seasoning
- 1 lb. flank steak or flat iron steak
- 2 tbsp. olive oil
- Black pepper, for seasoning
- 4 c. romaine lettuce
- 4 c. arugula, 1-inch pieces
- 1 c. cherry tomatoes, cut in half
- 2 c. radicchio, 1-inch pieces
- 1/4 c. thinly sliced radish
- 1/2 c. thinly sliced cucumber
- 1/4 c. feta cheese
- 1 medium avocado, sliced or diced
- 1/4 c. diced red onion

Equipment:

- Instant-Read Thermometer
- Cast Iron Skillet
- Steak Salad

Instructions:

1. Whisk together the vinegar, mustard, mayonnaise, salt, and pepper in a medium mixing bowl. Gently whisk in the olive

oil until the dressing thickens and emulsifies.

2. Pat the meat dry with paper towels. Season both sides with salt and pepper.

3. Preheat a large cast-iron skillet over high heat. When the oil is hot, add the steak and press it down. Cook for 4 minutes or until the top is browned.

4. Cook for 3 to 5 minutes, or until the steak reaches an internal temperature of 120 to 125°F (49 to 52 °C) for medium-rare.

5. Set the steak aside on a cutting board for 10 minutes. Cut the meat into 14-inch thick pieces perpendicular to the grain. Make it smaller if desired.

6. Combine the arugula, romaine, and radicchio in a large serving bowl. Add tomatoes, cucumber, radish, onion, sirloin, avocado, and feta cheese to the salad. Drizzle the balsamic vinaigrette over the steak salad.

BLT Sandwich

A sandwich made with bacon, lettuce, tomato, and mayonnaise.

Total Time: 20 minutes | Servings: 1

Ingredients:

- 2 slices of high-quality sandwich bread,
- 1 c. finely shredded iceberg lettuce
- Freshly ground black pepper
- 3 strips of thick-cut, naturally cured bacon
- 2 to 4 thick slices of ripe tomato
- Coarse sea salts
- 2 tbsp. mayonnaise

Special Equipment:

A griddle or large cast iron skillet, a bacon press, or a masonry trowel are all useful tools.

Instructions:

1. In a griddle or skillet over medium-low heat, melt the butter. To keep the bacon flat as it cooks, place it on top of a bacon press, skillet, or masonry trowel. Cook until the first side of the bacon is lightly browned, about 5 minutes, then flip, cover, and cook until the bacon is browned on both sides and the fat has rendered. Place the bacon on a platter lined with paper towels and set aside.

2. Toast the bread in the bacon fat over medium-low heat, stirring occasionally, until both sides are evenly brown.

3. On a work surface, spread mayonnaise on both top faces of toasted bread. Divide the lettuce between the two slices of bread. Season tomato slices with coarse salt and freshly ground pepper to taste on 1 piece of bread.

4. Cut the bacon slices in half and stack them in two layers of three half slices each on the sandwich, switching the orientation of the bacon in each layer for structural stability.

5. Close the sandwich and cut it in half diagonally. Serve immediately.

Hot Dogs

A frankfurter sausage served in a hot dog bun, often with toppings such as ketchup, mustard, and onions.

Ingredients:

- 1 c. all-purpose flour
- 1/4 tsp. salt
- 1 c. yellow cornmeal
- 1/4 c. granulated sugar
- 1 qt. vegetable oil
- 1/4 tsp. black pepper
- 4 tsp. baking powder

- 2 packages of frankfurters
- 1 egg
- 1 c. milk
- 16 wooden skewers or popsicle sticks

Instructions:

1. Combine cornmeal, flour, salt, pepper, sugar, and baking powder in a medium mixing bowl. Mix in the eggs and milk until well combined.
2. In a large frying pan over medium heat, heat the oil. Insert the frankfurters with wooden skewers. Dip the frankfurters into the batter and coat evenly.
3. Fry 2 or 3 corn dogs until golden brown, about 3 minutes. Using paper towels, pat dry.

Buffalo Wings

Chicken wings are breaded and fried, then coated in a spicy sauce.

Ingredients:

- 1 1/2 c. water
- 3 tbsp. cornstarch
- 1 c. flour
- 2 lb. chicken wing segments
- Vegetable oil for frying
- 2/3 c. gochujang sauce
- 1 tbsp. hardcore Carnivore Amplify (optional)
- 2 tbsp. rice vinegar
- 1/4 c. soy sauce

Instructions:

1. In a deep fryer or large heavy-bottomed saucepan, heat the oil to 375°F. Place a sheet pan lined with paper towels on a wire

rack.

2. In a mixing bowl, combine the flour, cornstarch, and water. Using a whisk, thoroughly combine all ingredients.

3. Dip a wing into the batter with tongs, then remove and place in the hot oil, allowing excess batter to drip off. Repeat with the opposite wing half. You may need to do this in three batches if you have a small fryer or pot. After 7 minutes, remove the wings to a cooling rack to cool. Continue with the rest of the wings, ensuring the oil has cooled to room temperature between batches.

4. Place the wings back in the oil and fry for another 5 minutes or until they are a deep golden brown. Set aside at least 2-3 minutes after returning to the rack.

5. Combine the gochujang, soy sauce, and vinegar in a large mixing bowl while the wings cool. Whisk everything together to make a sauce. To coat the wings, toss them in the sauce in the basin. Serve immediately.

Pulled Pork Sandwich

Shredded pork is cooked with BBQ sauce and served on a bun.

Ingredients:

- 1 (4 lb.) pork shoulder roast
- 1 tsp. vegetable oil
- 1/2 c. apple cider vinegar
- 1 c. barbeque sauce
- 1/2 c. chicken broth
- 1 tbsp. prepared yellow mustard
- 1/4 c. light brown sugar
- 1 tbsp. Worcestershire sauce
- 1 extra large onion, chopped

- 1 1/2 tsp. dried thyme
- 1 tbsp. chili powder
- 2 large cloves of garlic, crushed
- 2 tbsp. butter, or as need
- 8 hamburger buns, split

Equipment:

- Slow cooker

Instructions:

1. Fill the slow cooker halfway with vegetable oil. Pour the pork roast, barbecue sauce, vinegar, and chicken broth into the slow cooker. Add brown sugar, yellow mustard, Worcestershire sauce, chili powder, onion, garlic, and thyme. Cook on low for 10 to 12 hours or high for 5 to 6 hours or until pork shreds easily with a fork.
2. Using two forks, shred the pork from the slow cooker. Return the shredded pork to the slow cooker, along with the liquids.
3. Spread butter inside both hamburger bun halves. Heat the buns in a skillet, butter side down, until golden brown. Put pulled pork on toasted buns.

Hopefully, these recipes will be useful when planning your daily meal on the carnivore diet.

Meal Planning and Preparation Tips

How to Plan and Prepare Dinners for the Week?

Your knife skills won't be of much use without a plan. Esteemed chefs excel at multiple levels of menu planning, precise ingredient ordering, and the most efficient use of labor. Cooks prepare sauces, chop vegetables, and cook food that will be ready to serve by the end of the day.

If you aspire to eat healthier, meal preparation is crucial. By stocking your pantry and refrigerator with items that align with your strategy, you'll set yourself up for success.

Most shoppers purchase the same items repeatedly. If you wish to eat healthier or save money on prepared foods, planning is a must.

Make Room for Flexibility

Cooking for yourself enables you to do things your way. Do you prefer to improvise or follow a recipe? If you're new to meal planning, start by preparing the basics for three or four meals.

Do the Math

Review your weekly schedule. How many days will you be home for breakfast? Why not aim for all seven? Take note of that number. Select a day to cook. Do you have four hours available on a Saturday? You should be able to prepare your essentials, a sauce, a dressing, and maybe a dessert.

The Foundation: Establish a Pantry

You can do some improvising in your pantry to assist you in planning your meals. Sauces can be made during the meal preparation process or purchased and stored. You can also use frozen vegetables instead of prepping them on the day.

Canned salmon and tuna are ideal for a quick lunch or dinner.

Pesto, salad dressings, curry pastes, simmer sauces, salsa, soy sauce, Asian marinades, and spicy sauce are all excellent to have on hand.

Keep your family's preferred frozen vegetables in stock since they are already cooked.

As a treat, serve frozen tortellini or ravioli. Cook and combine with cooked meats and vegetables, as well as canned sauce.

Hard cheeses like Parmesan or Cheddar keep well and only need to be sprinkled on pasta or vegetables.

Meat, seafood, beans, and tofu are all examples of protein preps.

White rice, quinoa, and bulgur only take 15 minutes to cook.

Soups can be quickly made using boxed stocks and pre-cut meats and vegetables.

Plan to prepare protein portions for four meals—the easiest approach is to roast chicken, beef, fish, or sliced, marinated tofu in the oven, then distribute it among four containers.

Your Essential Preparation

Depending on what you're cooking, boil or bake it to make a quick salad, reheat it in a curry sauce, or microwave it on prep day.

Your primary preparation will be vegetables.

Vegetables: Roasted, par-cooked, and chopped vegetables for stir-frying or steaming.

In the winter, preheat the oven to roast your meats and a pan or two of your favorite roasted vegetables for the week. Caramelized Brussels sprouts, carrots, cauliflower, and other favorites can be stored and reheated for up to a week in the oven.

In the summer, simply chop your vegetables and store them in zip-top bags to steam, stir fry, or eat raw.

Salads and dressings are the foundation of your meal preparation.

Salad greens should be made or purchased for each meal. Pre-washed greens are available in 4-5 ounce packs, which is enough for four side salads.

Making salad dressings saves money and gives you more control over the ingredients. This can be as easy as shaking olive oil, vinegar, and crushed garlic in a jar or as complicated as creating a creamy yogurt or tahini dressing to last the week. You'll be more likely to eat your salad with a tasty dressing.

How to Cook Perfectly Grilled Steak

You can dress up your meal, prep salads, or make a nice evening supper with this quick and easy dish. The thinner the steak, the faster it will reach the ideal medium rare temperature.

This is the solution if your steaks are constantly sticking to the grill!

Keep the spices simple for a good steak. Salt and pepper are always required. For a little extra flavor, add some fresh rosemary to the mix.

You can easily omit the butter, but the melted butter at the end is believed to add moisture to the steak. Allow it to sit on the steaks while they rest.

Warm Up the Grill

Turn on your grill and allow it to heat up to medium-high. You can use a gas or charcoal grill for cooking. Reduce the heat to medium for the steaks and place them on the grill. Set them at an angle to get the best char marks.

Steaks Should Be Oiled

Brush both sides of the steaks with olive oil. This keeps the steaks from sticking to the grill and ruining the lovely char!

Season the Steaks

Season the steaks with salt, pepper, and fresh rosemary.

Examine the Temperature

Grill the steaks for 4 minutes per side until the internal temperature reaches 130°F/55°C for a medium-rare steak.

Finish with Butter

When the steaks are done, place them on a plate and top them with a pat of butter. Wrap the platter in foil and set aside the steaks to rest while the butter melts.

Clean the Grill

The first step toward a perfectly cooked steak is to clean the grates! This lets you turn your steaks more easily and eliminates the burned flavor. Flipping will be much easier if the grates are oiled.

Let the Steaks Come to Room Temperature

This may seem risky, but it allows the steaks to cook faster in the center! Set your steaks on the counter for about 30 minutes while you prepare your supper.

Increase the Taste

This quick and easy steak recipe yields wonderfully juicy and tasty results every time. Try a marinade or more garlic and herbs to add extra taste!

Steak Doneness Chart

Steak temperatures to aim for:

- Rare: 120-130 °F or 49-54 °C
- Medium Rare: 130-135 °F or 54-57 °C
- Medium: 135-145 °F or 57-63 °C
- Medium Well: 145-155 °F or 63-68 °C
- Well Done: 155 °F plus or 68 °C plus

For safety, the USDA advises cooking steaks to at least 145 °F .

Tips for Cooking and Serving Chicken Breasts

Have a Good Understanding of the Chicken Breast

Boneless chicken breasts are more popular than bone-in chicken breasts and thighs because they cook faster. They are frequently found skinless, making them slimmer than their bone-in cousin, usually seen with the skin on. Of course, boneless chicken breasts are delicious by themselves. However, recipes containing chicken bits or shreds, such as salads, stews, soups, or casseroles, are preferable. That's not to say you can't cook a bone-in chicken breast and cut around the bone afterward.

The main advantage of bone-in chicken breasts is that the flesh is juicier and tender. The rib bone is kept connected, which aids in the uniform transfer of heat and the production of the desired soft meat. This is why it is more likely to appear on the menu of a fine dining establishment.

Because of the fatty skin, bone-in chicken breasts are less lean than boneless, but the skin adds flavor and seals moisture in the bone-in option—think of it as a protective barrier. They are also less expensive than boneless chicken breasts, which must be processed more thoroughly. Bone-in chicken breasts, which can be served whole or chopped, are an excellent choice for taking center stage.

Easiest Ways to Cook Chicken Breasts—Including Grilled, Fried, and More

Chicken dinner, chicken meat! There's a reason it has a catchphrase. Chicken is easy to prepare and cook, and chicken breasts are a popular choice in many kitchens because they cook quickly and are lean. Chicken breasts are versatile and can be dressed up or down for a dinner party or a weekday meal.

They're ideal for meal prep and pre-packaged lunches. When cooked properly, chicken breasts are juicy and succulent. The disadvantage is that overcooking may cause them to dry out quickly, but if you're careful, cooking chicken breasts at home will yield excellent results every time.

Poach Chicken Breasts

Cooking the breasts gently in barely simmering water with a few seasonings keeps the flesh moist and soft without adding fat. Add sliced lemon, carrot, and celery slices, or half a yellow onion to boost the flavor. Both bone-in and boneless options are acceptable.

Grill Chicken Breasts

The key to tender grilled chicken breasts is to pound them to an even thickness. Begin with boneless, skinless chicken breasts, and you'll be done soon. Ideal for summer cookouts or a quick weeknight meal.

Fry Chicken Breasts

The only way to fry delicious chicken breasts is to coat them in seasoned breadcrumbs. Serve them on their own with a squeeze of lemon, on top of a salad, or as the foundation for a filling sandwich or chicken Parmesan. The oil temperature should be between 350 and 360°F if you have a deep-fry thermometer.

Meal Plans and Menus for the Carnivore Diet

30-Day Carnivore Diet Sample Meal Plans

Week 1

Day	Breakfast	Lunch	Dinner
Monday	Grilled Ribeye Steak (8 Oz.)	Slow Roast Topside Of Beef (12 Oz.)	Slow Roast Topside Of Beef (12 Oz.)
Tuesday	Grilled Ground Beef Burger Patty (8 Oz.)	Bbq Beef Ribs (240z.)	Bbq Sirloin Steak (12 Oz.)
Wednesday	Grilled Ground Beef Burger Patty (8 Oz.)	Bbq Beef Ribs (240z.)	Bbq Sirloin Steak (12 Oz.)
Thursday	Grilled Ground Beef Burger Patty (8 Oz.)	Bbq Ground Beef Burger Patty	Bbq Beef Ribs (24 Oz.)
Friday	Grilled Ground Beef Burger Patty (8 Oz.) Slow-Cooked Beef	Bbq Ribeye Steak (12 Oz.)	Grilled Porterhouse Steak (12 Oz.)

| Saturday | Grilled Sirloin Steak (8 Oz.) | Bbq Ribeye Steak (12 Oz.) | Bbq Beef Ribs (24 Oz.) |
| Sunday | Grilled Ground Beef Burger Patty (8 Oz.) | Patty (8 Oz.) Roasted Beef | Bbq Beef Ribs (24 Oz.) |

Week 2

Day	Breakfast	Lunch	Dinner
Monday	2 Grilled Chicken Breasts With 4 Pork Chops Fried Or Grilled	Grilled Trout Fillets (16 Oz.)	Slow Roast Topside Of Beef (12 Oz.)
Tuesday	3 Sausages (5 Oz.)	Roasted Pork Belly (10 Oz.)	Slow Roast Topside Of Beef (12 Oz.)
Wednesday	2 Grilled Chicken Breasts	2 Grilled Chicken Breasts With 4pork Chops- Fried Or Grilled	"Slow Roast Topside Of Beef (12 Oz.)
Thursday	Grilled Ground Beef Burger Patty (8 Oz.) With Cheese	The Bone (15 Oz.) With Butter	Slow Roast Topside Of Beef (12 Oz.)
Friday	2 Grilled Chicken Breasts	Roast Salmon Cutlets (15 Oz.) With Butter	Grilled Ribeye Steak (12 Oz.)

Saturday	Grilled Pork Sausages (5 Oz.)	2 Grilled Chicken Breasts With 4 pork Chops Fried Or Grilled	Slow Roast Topside Of Beef (12 Oz.)
Sunday	Grilled Ground Beef Burger Patty (8 Oz.) With Cheese	Roasted Pork Belly (10 Oz.)	Grilled Ribeye Steak (12 Oz.)

Week 3

Day	Breakfast	Lunch	Dinner
Monday	Grilled Ribeye steak (8 Oz)	3 Grilled Chicken Breasts	Grilled Ribeye Steak (8 Oz.) Roasted Beef Liver (4 Oz.)
Tuesday	5 Slices Of Bacon (4 Oz.) 1-2 100% Pork Sausages (3 Oz.)	Roast Salmon Cutlets On The Bone(15 Oz.)	Grilled Ground Beefburger
Wednesday	Grilled Sirloin Steak (8 Oz.)	Roast Salmon Cutlets On The Bone(15 Oz.)	4 pork Chops Fried Or Grilled
Thursday	2 Grilled Chicken Breasts With Slow Roast Topside Of Beef (12 Oz.)	Roast Salmon Cutlets	Grilled Ribeye Steak (8 Oz.) Roasted Beef Liver (4 Oz.)
Friday	Grilled Ribeye Steak (12 Oz.)	Slow Roast Topside Of Beef (12 Oz.)	Grilled Ground Beefburger

| Saturday | 5 Slices Of Bacon (4 Oz.) 1-2 100% Pork Sausages (3 Oz.) | Roast Salmon Cutlets On The Bone(15 Oz.) | 4 Fresh Lamb Chops (12 Oz.) |
| Sunday | Grilled Sirloin Steak (8 Oz.) | Roast Salmon Cutlets On The Bone(15 Oz.) | Grilled Sirloin Steak (12 Oz.) |

Week 4

Day	Breakfast	Lunch	Dinner
Monday	Grilled Ground Beefburger	Grilled Ground Beef Burger Patty (12 Oz.)	4 pork Chops Fried Or Grilled (12 Oz.)
Tuesday	Grilled Beef (Grounded)Burger	Grilled Ribeye Steak (8 Oz.)	4 pork Chops Fried Or Grilled (12 Oz.)
Wednesday	Grilled Ribeye Steak (8 Oz.)	Grilled Ground Beef Burger Patty (12 Oz.)	Fatty Fish Cutlets On The Bone (15 Oz.)
Thursday	Grilled Ribeye Steak (8 Oz.)	Grilled Ground Beef Burger Patty (12 Oz.)	Slow Roast Topside Of Beef (12 Oz.)
Friday	Grilled Beef (Grounded) Burger	Grilled Ground Beef Burger Patty (12 Oz.)	Grilled Porterhouse Steak (12 Oz.)
Saturday	Grilled Ribeye Steak (8 Oz.)	Roasted Beefliver (4 Oz.)	Grilled Porterhouse Steak (12 Oz.)

Sunday	Grilled Ribeye Steak (8 Oz.)	Grilled Ribeye Steak (8 Oz.)	Slow Roast topside of Beef Kidney (4 Oz.)

Customized Meal Plans for Special Dietary Needs

Meal Plan for Lowering Cholesterol and Balancing Saturated Fats

Learn how to lower your high cholesterol and improve your heart health by following this simple 3-day low-cholesterol meal plan for beginners.

Day 1

Breakfast - 280 calories

- 1 serving of Cinnamon Roll Overnight Oats
- 1 5-oz. container of nonfat plain Greek yogurt

Breakfast Snack - 206 calories

- 1/4 cup of unsalted dry-roasted almonds

Lunch - 428 calories

- 1 clementine
- Kale and Chicken Salad along with Peanut Dressing
- 1 serving of Sweet Potato

Lunch Snack - 112 calories

- 1/4 cup hummus
- 1/2 cup cucumber, sliced

Dinner - 472 calories

- 1 serving of Stuffed Sweet Potato along with Hummus Dressing

Daily Totals: 85 g protein, 1,497 calories, 184 g carbohydrates, 52g fat, 42g fiber, 1,664mg sodium, 7g saturated fat

To acquire 1,200 calories, substitute 1/4 cup of sliced bell pepper for the breakfast snack and leave out the hummus for the noon snack.

To get to 2,000 calories, do the following: 1 large apple for breakfast, 1 large pear for breakfast snack, 1 cup nonfat, regular Greek yogurt for lunch, and 1 serve Guacamole Chopped Salad for supper.

Day 2

Breakfast - 280 calories

- 1 serving of Cinnamon Roll Overnight Oats
- 1 5-oz. container of nonfat plain Greek yogurt

Breakfast Snack - 131 calories

- 1 large pear

Lunch - 428 calories

- 1 clementine
- 1 serving of Sweet Potato, Kale, and Chicken Salad Plus Peanut Dressing

Lunch Snack - 197 calories

- 1/4 cup raspberries
- 1 cup nonfat plain Greek yogurt
- 1 Tbsp. chopped walnuts

Dinner - 450 calories

- 1 serving of Turkey and Sweet Potato Chili
- 1 serving of Guacamole Chopped Salad

Daily Totals: 96 g protein, 1,486 calories, 33g fiber, 158g carbohydrates, 1,623 mg sodium, 57g fat, 9 g saturated fat

To acquire 1,200 calories, modify the breakfast snack to one plum and leave out the yogurt and chopped walnuts at lunch.

To get to 2,000 calories, do three tablespoons of chopped walnuts for the morning, ⅓ cup unsalted dry-roasted almonds for breakfast snack, and a 1-ounce slice of whole-wheat bread for supper.

Day 3

Breakfast - 293 calories

- 1 serving of Apple & Peanut Butter Toast

Snack - 131 calories

- 1 large pear

Lunch - 387 calories

- 1 medium orange
- 1 serving Veggie and Hummus Sandwich

Snack - 206 calories

- 1/4 cup of unsalted dry-roasted almonds

Dinner - 504 calories

- 1 serving Sheet-Pan Salmon along with Sweet Potatoes & Broccoli

Daily Totals: 1,521 calories, 153g carbohydrates, 67 g protein, 37 g fiber, 12 g saturated fat, 76g fat, 1,257 mg sodium

To acquire 1,200 calories, modify the breakfast snack to 1 clementine, leave out the orange at lunch, and replace it with 1 plum.

To consume 2,000 calories: Add ⅓ of walnut halves to breakfast. Lunch should include 1 cup of nonfat plain Greek yogurt and 1 big apple as a snack.

Vegetarian and Vegan Meal Plans

Vegan Diet Fundamentals and How to Begin

A vegan diet is a plant-based diet that excludes all animal products, including meat, fish, dairy, and honey. The vegetarian diet excludes meat and fish but allows for dairy and eggs.

To reap the benefits of this eating plan, focus on nutrient-dense whole foods like beans, lentils, nuts, seeds, whole grains, and plenty of fruits and vegetables.

Try to incorporate protein foods such as peanut butter, beans, lentils, tofu, seitan, and pecans into the majority of your meals to keep you satisfied between meals. If the vegan diet seems overwhelming, start with a couple of meatless days per week and work your way up.

What Can Be Eaten on a Vegan Diet

- Edamame
- Beans
- Tofu
- Lentils
- Soy
- Whole grains (oatmeal, quinoa, brown rice, wheat bread)
- Nuts, seeds, and nut kinds of butter
- Seitan

- Fruits
- Avocado
- Tempeh
- Vegetables
- Coconut
- Olives and olive oil
- Nutritional Yeast

Sample Meal Plan

Here's a one-week meal plan that includes some healthful items that may be eaten on a vegan diet.

Day	Breakfast	Lunch	Dinner	Snacks
Monday	Potato Toast Spiced With Peanut Butter & Banana	Tempeh Taco Salad With Quinoa, Avocados, Beans, Onions, Tomatoes, And Cilantro	Oat Risotto With Swiss Chard, Mushrooms, And Butternut Squash	Vegan Protein Shake, Mixed Berries, And Walnuts
Tuesday	Broccoli, Tomatoes, Eggless Quiche With Silken Tofu, And Spinach	Chickpea & Spinach Curry With Brown Rice	Olives, Peppers, Mediterranean Lentil Salad With Cucumbers, Sun-Dried Tomatoes, Kale, And Parsley	Sliced Pear, Chia Seeds, Roasted Edamame, And Energy Balls Made From Oats, Nut Butter, And Dried Fruit
Wednesday	Avocado, Tempeh Bacon With Sautéed Mushrooms And Wilted Arugula	A Side Salad And Whole-Grain Pasta With Lentil "Meatballs"	Cauliflower And Chickpea Tacos, Along With Guacamole And Pico De Gallo	Kale Chips, Trail Mix, And Air-Popped Popcorn
Friday	Oats With Apple Slices, Pumpkin Seeds,	Black Bean Veggie Burger Along With	Collard Greens, Mac And "Cheese" Along	Coconut Chia Pudding And Granola,

	Cinnamon, And Nut Butter	Steamed Broccoli & Sweet Potato Wedges	With Nutritional Yeast	Pistachios
Saturday	Whole-Grain Toast And Nutritional Yeast Alongside A Vegan Protein Shake	Baked Potato And Lentil Chili With Grilled Asparagus	Tomatoes, Onions, Vegetable Paella With Brown Rice, Artichoke, And Chickpeas	Almonds, Fruit Salad, And Carrots With Hummus
Sunday	Tomatoes, Breakfast Skillet With Tempeh, Broccoli, Kale, And Zucchini	Garlic-Ginger Tofu Along With Stir-Fried Veggies And Quinoa	Corn, And Bean Salad, Bell Peppers, Tomatoes, And Onions	Frozen Grapes, And Celery, Along With Almond Butter

FAQs about the Carnivore Diet and Lifestyle

1. What Can Be Eaten on The Carnivore Diet?

Beef, chicken, pork, lamb, bison, turkey, and other seafood are examples of meats that can be eaten on the carnivore diet. Other animal products include eggs, lard, bone marrow, bone broth, fat, cheese, and milk.

2. Is the Carnivore Diet Safe?

The carnivore diet is safe; many societies worldwide eat only meat yearly.

3. Can You Lose Weight on the Carnivore Diet?

Many people lose weight after starting a carnivorous diet. You may notice changes in your weight, appetite, energy, and other areas as your body adjusts to the new diet. Getting into ketosis and putting your body into fat-burning mode can aid in weight loss and usually allows dieters to lose weight quickly.

4. Will the Carnivore Diet Cause Deficiencies in Nutrients?

An all-meat diet will not result in nutrient deficiencies if you vary your low-carb diet. You still need a lot of minerals and vitamins for your immune and digestive systems, but by including fish and shellfish on your carnivore diet food list, you can get these nutrients while avoiding stomach problems.

5. How Long Will It Take to Adapt to the Carnivore Diet?

It takes about a week to adjust to the carnivorous diet and enter full ketosis. Depending on how disciplined you are and how much you exercise, this could take up to two weeks.

6. Does a Carnivore Diet Put One in Ketosis?

The carnivore diet usually gets you into ketosis in 5 to 10 days. A carnivorous lifestyle, such as the ketogenic diet, eliminates almost all carb intake, leaving your body more reliant on fat and protein for energy.

7. Is a Carnivore Diet Expensive?

The carnivorous diet is undoubtedly expensive, but there are excellent ways to cut costs. You can still eat grass-fed beef daily if you choose cheaper cuts.

8. Does a Carnivore Diet Improves Testosterone?

Research on high-fat and low-fiber consumption shows that the carnivore diet can boost testosterone levels. However, remember that other health issues will also impact your testosterone levels.

9. How Long Will It Take For a Carnivore Diet to Work?

Everyone is different regarding adopting the carnivore diet and reaping the fantastic benefits. Some people see results in days, while others may take years to recover from physical trauma. Most people have fully adjusted and are reaping the benefits of the carnivorous diet after six months.

10. Any Difference Between the Keto and Carnivore Diets?

The main difference between the ketogenic and carnivore diets is that the keto diet allows certain carbs/fiber/plant-based meals while the carnivore diet does not. The keto diet allows for consuming berries, nuts, and other low-carb plant foods. On the other hand, the carnivore diet prohibits any animal-derived items.

How to Overcome Common Challenges

For many years, studies have linked red meat diets to cardiovascular disease, diabetes, and other negative side effects. This all-meat diet is one of the most limited options.

Adaptation Period Symptoms

It will take some time for your body to adjust to the nutritional, hormonal, and intestinal changes caused by the complete elimination of most food categories.

Throughout the adaptation phase, many unfavorable symptoms and side effects will occur.

Nausea and flu are the most common transient side effects, but they usually go away after 2-4 weeks. Cognitive fog, impatience, cravings, poor attention, and headaches are other symptoms to expect during the adjustment period.

Tips for Staying Motivated and On Track

Consume plenty of water. Here are two additional easy strategies to help lessen, if not eliminate, the majority of your discomfort while you adjust to the carnivorous diet:

Consuming More Meat

A carnivore diet is often high in fat and protein, so you'll feel full for a long time. This may deceive you into eating very little, and therein lies the problem.

One of the main reasons 'carnivores' suffer is that they eat infrequently. It is common to experience extreme hunger during the first few weeks; the last thing you want to do is ignore it.

To satisfy your hunger, eat more meat or higher-quality cuts. Instead of worrying about gaining weight, figure out how many calories you need and use that number to determine food portions.

Supplements for Electrolyte Support

When glycogen stores are broken down to release energy, you will lose weight in the first few days—weight loss is natural when you don't eat carbohydrates. This process removes a significant amount of water and sodium, chloride, potassium, and magnesium, all of which must be replaced. But how precisely? Increase your salt intake.

Drink meaty bone broth to replenish water and add salt and potassium, which will help alleviate some of the discomfort. If this doesn't work, you may need an electrolyte supplement to mineralize yourself.

Additional tablets are especially important if magnesium or potassium are depleted. The optimum daily values for various deficiencies are 2-7g sodium, 0.25-0.5g magnesium, and 0.5-3.5g potassium.